MD
MAPPING

Plot your way to emotional health and happiness

DR LIZ MILLER

RODALE

First published 2009 by Rodale

This edition published 2011 by Rodale
an imprint of Pan Macmillan, a division of Macmillan Publishers Limited
Pan Macmillan, 20 New Wharf Road, London N1 9RR
Basingstoke and Oxford
Associated companies throughout the world
www.panmacmillan.com

ISBN 978-1-9057-4477-0

9 8 7 6 5 4 3 2 1

A CIP catalogue record for this book is available from the British Library.

Printed in the UK by CPI Mackays, Chatham ME5 8TD

Visit **www.panmacmillan.com** to read more about all our books
and to buy them. You will also find features, author interviews and
news of any author events, and you can sign up for e-newsletters
so that you're always first to hear about our new releases.

LIVE YOUR WHOLE LIFE

We inspire and enable people to improve their lives and the world around them

Dedication

To all those who are mental health patients. It is time for a better deal, without the stigma and discrimination that makes life that bit more difficult.

And to my partner, MQ, for being the best.

Acknowledgements

Thank you to Liz Gough for believing in me from day one and for understanding the potential power of MoodMapping. Thanks are also due to her for being as patient as an editor can be and still run a business . . . My thanks to project editor Gill Paul who has been a complete star and without whose efforts this book would not exist. Finally, thanks to everyone who has so willingly shared their time and their experiences, upon which this book is based, especially the Tuesday night group.

Contents

Foreword

Mood disorders are among the most distressing diseases from which to suffer. *MoodMapping: Plot Your Way to Emotional Health and Happiness* is an excellent resource for sufferers. In this clearly written book, the author, herself a sufferer, describes how she devised MoodMapping, which is a powerful new technique allowing the self-assessment and self-monitoring of mood. It is interesting that rather than being conceived by a psychiatrist, it took the genius and training of a brilliant neurosurgeon to devise this method.

Dr Liz Miller describes how those who suffer from a mood disorder can apply her technique successfully to cope with the vicissitudes of life. Her writing is brilliant, open and honest. She makes it very easy to follow her method, in a text that is rich in practical examples. Dr Miller displays a profound understanding of the daily difficulties that patients encounter in the personal arena of their own thoughts. She explains how the gladiatorial battles taking place there can be won, with negative thoughts and emotions being vanquished.

This book is truly a delight to read. I highly recommend it.

Professor Basant K. Puri
MA, PhD, MB, BChir, BSc (Hons) MathSci,
MRCPsych, DipStat, PG Cert Maths, MMath.
Hammersmith Hospital
Imperial College London

Co-author of *The Natural Way to Beat Depression.*

Introduction

This book is for people with moods – in particular, people with mood problems. It is for those of us who know what we should be doing but can't always manage it, because we simply don't feel like doing it. The book is designed to help those of us who have difficulty managing our moods, and whose moods tend to dictate the pattern of our lives.

Whether this is your first self-development book or whether you are further down the road, it will help you to think and feel differently about yourself and the people around you. You may have had a medical diagnosis pinpointing the cause of your mood problems, and you may even be taking medication. Equally, however, you may simply be aware that your moods are out of control, and want to live your life in a more positive, productive way. MoodMapping can help you to get back in control, and the strategies described in this book are suitable for people of *all* ages.

MoodMapping is not intended to be a fix-all for serious mental health problems, or a substitute for medication or counselling. Instead, it will provide you with alternative ways to make your life easier, take the edge off anxiety, depression or anything else that hampers the way you live, and help to create a better life for you and the people around you.

And there's more! MoodMapping can help you to achieve peak performance, because the very same strategies that can help someone who struggles to get up in the morning can help you to achieve excellence. Moods affect our performance from day to day and week to week. If you positively manage your moods, you will improve your performance, from moment to moment and from year to year.

This book offers advice and strategies, and provides an alternative way to understand yourself and how you think, feel and behave. Even the most seasoned self-developers will find something new, useful and engaging in its pages. If you want to live a healthier life but can't always do what you know you should, this book offers you a new approach. If you want a richer and more fulfilled life – to feel and get on better with the people around you – it offers key insights and steps to reach that goal. Whether you manage people, work as part of a team, have a family, or are involved in a relationship, this book will help you to get more out of life. It gives you practical tips backed up by a new, different and proven viewpoint. There is no other book like this. MoodMapping is not a quick fix, because habits and problems that you spent years acquiring will not go away overnight. But this book is a first step to the life that you want to lead.

How can MoodMapping help?

MoodMapping is a skill that provides a new way of understanding and managing moods. Some people find it easier than others but everyone, by learning a few simple strategies, can start to manage their moods. MoodMapping is a practical tool backed up with practical suggestions to help you feel better, healthier and more in control of your life. In fact, the key to consistent energy and feeling good is ensuring that your moods are under control. By learning to understand and master them, we can be 'captain of our soul' and 'master of our fate'. What's more, once you learn to manage your own moods, you can help the people around you to manage theirs – your children, your partner, your friends, your team, and the people who come to you for advice.

This book brings together my own experience and the experience of the people with whom I work and teach. MoodMapping works! I have experienced the benefits on a personal level, as has every other person who has adopted it. I have seen people's lives –

and those of their friends and families – transformed, as everyone becomes involved in the process of mood control. I've written this book because I know that you, too, will benefit from the greater self-awareness, self-knowledge and better self-management that come from regularly mapping your mood.

The benefits are utterly life-enhancing, including improved creativity, self-esteem and a calmer and more manageable life. Mood-Mapping helps you get rid of your worst anxieties and gives you greater freedom to do what you want with your time – and to be successful in those areas of life that are important to you.

What is mood?

We all have moods all of the time. Moods and mood disorders dominate people's lives. There has been plenty written already about 'mood disorders', such as anxiety and depression, and even bipolar disorder. By contrast, there are almost no books about 'mood order'. And that's what this book is all about.

Moods are an internal measure of how we are. We do not express our moods directly. Instead, we express them indirectly in the way we think, communicate, behave and see the world. Moods are different from emotions, which are directly expressed or suppressed. So, for example, when someone is angry, he or she can either shout and lash out or suppress their anger and seethe quietly. Almost all anger reflects an underlying irritable, anxious mood. This mood has provided the soil that allowed the emotion of anger to grow.

By comparison, if someone is experiencing a happy and calm mood, it is much harder to become angry, to panic, or to be stressed. This 'indirectness' is perhaps the main reason why moods have been so little studied. MoodMapping provides the means to makes what is implicit, explicit. In other words, MoodMapping shows people where they are and what they can do about their mood, so that they do not have to wait until they get angry to take action. MoodMapping enriches the soil from which our emotions grow.

If you are an introvert – that is, someone with more of a quiet, shy nature – what you do or say tends to depend a lot upon how you feel. In other words, you are affected by your moods. On the other hand, extroverts, who focus more on the outside world, can more easily ignore their moods. However, extroverts who ignore how they feel for too long can lose sight of their deeper human needs. As a result, they become stressed, no longer enjoy life and find that they've lost their purpose. Whether you are inward- or outward-looking, you can manage your moods so that they work for you and ensure that your life is balanced and productive.

Moods can be managed, both in the immediate moment and in the longer term, and to begin with you'll need to understand the five key inputs to mood. These keys are your surroundings, your physical body, your relationships, your knowledge and your nature (or who you are). We'll look at these in more detail later on.

Whether you suffer from mood swings, depression, bipolar disorder, anxiety or PMS, or are just feeling stressed and 'on edge' – you can do something about it. You can learn how to manage your own mood so that you feel better, and you can manage the moods of the people around you as well. This is an incredible tool to have at your disposal. Whether you are at home with your children, at work with your colleagues, or meeting someone for the first time; whether you are in business and need to make sales, or a teacher or health professional, you can influence almost any situation by learning to manage your mood and those of others.

I learnt these strategies by first learning to manage my own moods. Now I teach others how to master their moods, so that they too can increase their happiness and well-being – and the happiness and well-being of the people around them. I believe mood is the most important and least considered part of our minds. Your mood reflects your energy. It is a meter that reveals whether you are calm and collected, or excitable and anxious. Your mood has more influence and impact on your day-to-day affairs than any other aspect of your psychology. With a good mood you can conquer the world; with a bad one you just want to crawl under the duvet and hide away from the world.

My personal experiences

My interest in mood-management stems from my own experience. At the age of 28, I was a young, up-and-coming neurosurgeon. I had almost finished my training, and had done research, passed examinations and was a regular speaker at international neuro-surgical conferences. One professor described me as 'the brightest young thing in neurosurgery this decade'.

And then, at 29, I was in a locked ward of the Edinburgh Royal Infirmary, sectioned under the Mental Health Act, my career in ruins. And because of my mental illness, I had no immediate hope of working in medicine again.

There were good reasons for being there. I was exhausted, iso-lated in my career and no longer able to work. I had also been diagnosed with bipolar disorder (see page 233 for more on this condition). I recovered and, 10 months later, was fit to return to work. I did get another job, largely thanks to favours from people whom my father knew. Nonetheless, as far as my mental health was concerned, I was in denial. If people asked why I left Edin-burgh, I made up a story about missing my family and moving to the south of England so that I could be closer to them. I told no one what had happened to me.

My family and I silently agreed not to talk about it. Two more mental health sections later, and I was still in denial. My ability to work was steadily worsening. I had gone from being a top-flight neurosurgeon to a locum GP. I smoked, and rarely exercised. Psy-chiatrists were treating me as if I were a creature that had crawled out from under a stone. They assumed that because I was a doc-tor, I knew what they meant by 'a manic-depressive psychotic ill-ness'. They also assumed that I understood the importance of tak-ing medication regularly and had enough knowledge to stay out of trouble. Since I kept turning up as a patient, I was obviously a deeply flawed human being, worthy only of their contempt.

Nonetheless, something inside me believed that it was possible to find the answer to this condition and that I was not destined to spend the rest of my life on tablets. Two films had a disproportion-ate influence. The first was *Shine*, the story of David Helfgott, an international pianist who developed schizophrenia. He spent many years in a mental hospital until he was finally discharged and started to play the piano again. I went to a concert he gave at the Royal Albert Hall, where I had (in a slightly manic mood) bought all the seats in the front row for friends. There were moments of genius and, at the end, I was the first on my feet to give him a well-earned standing ovation. He, perhaps more than anyone else, showed me that there is life after mental illness and above all you just need the courage to keep going. I still cry when I watch that film.

The other film was *Beautiful Mind,* with Russell Crowe as John Nash. More than any other film I've seen, it shows the reality of a psychotic delusion. From Nash's perspective his room is the nerve centre of a complicated operation that runs the military intelligence of the Western world, but to others, it looks like a frantic mess. Both films have happy endings, where the love of a beautiful woman helps the hero to find his salvation. I can vouch for the fact that strength and support from the people in your life can help you to come back from the other side.

During my third mental health section I was put in a ward with other doctors and health professionals in the Bethlem Royal Hospital in Kent, which is, perhaps, the last mental asylum left in England that maintains the Victorian concept of 'asylum' as a place of safety. It feels in many ways like my alma mater. Set in acres of beautiful woods and parkland with abundant wildlife, its natural background is healing. I have been back several times both to walk in the park and to visit the museum, which has an extensive collection of art.

By this stage, I knew that I had a serious problem. I had spent almost 18 months of my life in various psychiatric hospitals, and I was finding it harder to work in the way that I used to. My concentration was poor, and I was finding it difficult to grapple with complex problems. I could no longer see any kind of future in medicine and, under those circumstances, I finally accepted the diagnosis of bipolar disorder.

That was a bleak moment. I had always been proud of my brain, my ability to think on my feet, and to know what to do regardless of what was going on around me. The diagnosis of a mental-health condition goes to the heart of who you are. There is no escape from it. It says something about your identity that is not kind and not always helpful. And no matter *who* you are, it can come as a shock and undermine everything you believed about yourself. There was even a chance that the condition could kill me because there is a much higher-than-average rate of suicide in people with bipolar disorder. I sank into a depression that lasted two or three years and, at the time, I never expected to work again. Whenever I was on my own, I became overwhelmed and burst into tears.

Looking back, I can see that there were good reasons to deny that I had a mental-health problem. Denying my illness meant that I was able to get back to work and carry on as though nothing had happened. The medical profession assumes that doctors do not become ill – diseases are for patients, and doctors are different. This school of thought undoubtedly hampered my treatment and recovery, for when psychiatrists told me I was ill, I believed they were lying to me: I was a doctor and I couldn't get ill. If there is stigma and prejudice against mental illness in the outside world, it is ten times worse in the medical profession. A doctor in a mental asylum is like a policeman who gets sent to prison, or an accountant caught fiddling the books. The whole profession was in denial.

Nowadays mood disorders are talked about. It is no longer shameful to admit that you have had a problem with mental health or mood disorders. Indeed, we are experiencing a wave of interest in destigmatising mental health. Books explore mental health issues and TV documentaries show how it feels to have a mental health problem. I was lucky enough to take part in *The Secret Life of a Manic-Depressive* with Stephen Fry, in which I returned to Bethlem Royal Hospital to talk about how being sectioned and my subsequent recovery changed my approach to mental health. Exposures such as this make sure that we will never again enter the dark ages.

In 1998, when I was setting up the Doctors' Support Network with my colleague, Dr Soames Michelson, who suffered from depression, we visited various medical institutions, including the

British Medical Association and the Royal College of Psychiatrists. We were repeatedly told: 'Doctors don't have mental health problems. I think you'll find you are the only ones.' This approach wasn't helpful then, and didn't bode well for the future. Doctors are people, and it was time that this was accepted, and that the potential for ill-health was acknowledged.

Not only did the medical profession deny the extent of mental-health problems within the profession, but it also offered nothing to doctors with mental ill-health. If there was a whisper that you might not be 'of sound mind', you were immediately shown the door. The General Medical Council, the doctors' regulatory body, still considers mental ill-health to be a personal failing, similar to misconduct or poor work performance. It puts doctors 'on trial' in front of a quasi-judicial tribunal, with or without a lawyer, where they are expected to prove that they are of sound mind. At the beginning of the twenty-first century, such an old-fashioned approach to mental health ill becomes the medical profession.

It is therefore not surprising that, faced with these alternatives, one doctor a week commits suicide in the UK. I am pleased to say that, outside the General Medical Council, attitudes have changed. This is, perhaps, in some part due to the work of the Doctors' Support Network. Even so, there is still a lot more to be done before mental ill-health is given the same 'respect' as other illnesses.

Overcoming bipolar disorder

My story is not unique, but it is what makes this book unique. I have been there. Accepting I have had bipolar mood disorder has been the key to my own recovery and the events that have changed my life. I began my career as a doctor believing that if you couldn't stand the heat, you should get out of the kitchen and that medicine was an objective discipline with a scientific foundation. It took three nervous breakdowns to find out how wrong I could be.

My family and friends did not think that I should return to medicine. I had given my career just about everything I had. I had trained as a neurosurgeon, then in Accident and Emergency, and finally as a General Practitioner. It seemed that I became ill no matter what I did.

I married, but my marriage was not the success it might have been. My husband Richard gave me all the support he could and, given my mental state, we did as well as anyone could have. I now understand more about how mental ill-health can affect the lives of the people around the sufferer, and how even the best relationships can be blown apart in the maelstrom that surrounds it. In the early days, Richard was an essential member, if not the backbone, of the Doctors' Support Network. He helped stuff innumerable newsletters into envelopes and generously gave his time and hospitality to any number of strange-looking friends who came past.

But within a couple of years, I became restless and eventually moved out. I am delighted to say that Richard is now happily married to a beautiful lady. Me? I am living with the man of my dreams and together we are 'rewriting' medicine and trying to improve people's mental (and physical) health. Marriage had not cured my depression, and I don't expect it to.

During the time that I was married to Richard, I was deeply unhappy – if not suicidal. That unhappiness did not stem from my marriage – Richard went well beyond the call of duty – but from the fact that I could not see a future. I had spent the last 20 years of my life working all the hours there were, and I had nothing to show for it. I had been told I would be on medication for the rest of my life, that I was at constant risk of further episodes of mental illness, and that I would probably never work again. Nothing could survive in those bleak surroundings.

The first stage of acceptance was the hardest, something that is true of many life experiences. Until you have accepted what has happened, whether it is the loss of a limb, a loved one or a future you had planned, it is difficult to move forward. I grieved for what might have been – a glittering career as a neurosurgeon, a Nobel prize for describing the hypothalamic control of sodium metabolism, a consultant post in Accident and Emergency, and even the ability to work part-time in General Practice.

But it got easier. The second stage of understanding what had happened took longer, but it gave me hope. If I could get to grips with it, perhaps I could prevent it from happening again. Then, at least, I could stop my medication and get on with my life in a quiet, if unimpressive, way. This stage was dominated by my fear of becoming ill again. I went to bed early, I stopped listening to anything that might upset me, such as loud music and disturbing films, and spent my days quietly. I refused to travel outside Europe in case jet lag triggered another episode. And, largely because of Richard's prompting and bribery, I stopped smoking. I started running, and I read everything I could about bipolar disorder.

The first thing that struck me was how little was actually known about bipolar disorder. The drug Lithium was believed to be the only effective treatment. Although other drugs, such as Carbamezipine, Valproate and Lamotrigine, were also used to stabilise moods, it was not clear how any of them worked. There were shelves of books and scientific articles written about depression and schizophrenia, but there was almost nothing written about bipolar disorder. This has changed a great deal in the last ten to fifteen years; however, in those days, the only treatment for bipolar disorder was medication.

I did not find the answer I was looking for in medical literature, and it became clear that I needed to look elsewhere. I joined the Manic Depression Fellowship (now called the Bipolar Organisation) and Mary Fulford, the Chief Executive, gave me the chance to do some part-time voluntary work. My psychiatrist encouraged me to do so, but qualified it by saying 'Don't make a career out of it' – more medical advice I haven't taken! I worked with the Bipolar Organisation on their self-management programme, which is, I believe, the single greatest advance in the management of bipolar disorder since the introduction of Lithium. In the process, a light went on inside my head. I suddenly understood that it was possible to manage this condition, as long as I was aware of what was happening to me.

So, the first step was to understand how I felt. The Bipolar Organisation used a straightforward mood chart that recorded how good or bad you were feeling at any particular time. Realising that life was not that simple, I started a diary. I monitored exactly how much energy I had, how good or bad I felt, how much I spent, how much I slept, where I had been, who I talked to and for how long, how long I could concentrate for, and what happened to me during the day. In the beginning I spent most of my day recording what happened to me and how I felt. Every day I wrote numerous sheets of A4 describing my life and the way I saw it – how awful my parents were, how unfair life was, what I watched on the television, what music I listened to and what effect it had.

I started writing numerous novels, short stories and articles about my experiences. I contributed a column to *Pendulum*, the magazine of the Bipolar Organisation, describing in everyday language the latest scientific research on bipolar disorder. I was setting up the Doctors' Support Network, talking to people, having parties and writing. At that point, I was able to look at my life and realise that I was, actually, doing everything I wanted to do. I just wasn't getting paid for it. Luckily, Richard was wealthy enough to afford me.

I did eventually get back to paid work, starting back in General Practice and Occupational Health. Occupational Health looks at the relationship between health and work. My experience with doctors looking to return to work after mental illness was useful, while my work in Occupational Health meant I could offer the doctors advice about the Disability Discrimination Act and their employers' duty of care. And I continued my interest in my own and other peoples' mental health.

After the first few months of avidly writing a diary about how I felt and what had happened to me, I began to get a sense of how I was feeling. To people who naturally know how they feel, this may not seem exciting. But for someone like myself, who had never thought that personal feelings were important, it was a revelation. I began to see the links between what I did and how I felt, and I discovered that the most important part of my mood was how much energy I had and how positive or negative I was feeling. Too much alcohol, and I didn't just have a hangover but I also felt depressed. Bad news caused anxiety and good news made me feel better. Decorating the flat where we lived was a real boost. Exercise, such as swimming, made me feel better. It was from these insights that I developed MoodMapping. By writing down everything that affected my mood, and plotting my mood on a map, I began to see the five main keys to mood emerge.

Putting MoodMapping into practice

I started using MoodMapping with the Fire Service. Fire-fighters, like police and ambulance personnel, are on the front line of human tragedy. These men and women deal with the worst that can occur, 24 hours a day. As a result, it is not surprising that many fire-fighters have problems with their emotional health. One minute they may be sitting quietly in the mess, and 20 minutes later they are cutting people out of a multi-car pile-up. They experience many stressful events, and their work often disrupts their home lives making them more vulnerable to mental and physical health problems.

My job as an Occupational Health Physician with the Fire Service was the ideal setting to explore mental health. There was a relatively relaxed attitude to clinic times, so I could give people the time and attention they needed. These clinics were a unique opportunity to explore the minds and experiences of the fire-fighters I worked with, and help them to examine and establish new ways of getting their mental health on an even keel.

From here, I began running self-management workshops on MoodMapping for people with bipolar disorder. The response was very positive. Here was a simple tool that helped people understand how they felt, and it combined well with simple ways to change mood. MoodMapping is not the first chart to record moods, but it is the first map. It differentiates between the two parts of mood – energy and well-being – so that the low positive energy of calm can be distinguished from the low negative energy of depression. Equally, the high positive energy of action is differentiated from the high negative energy of anxiety. I was on to something!

In the meantime, I studied for a psychology degree at the Open

University and then an MSc in Organisational Psychology at Birkbeck College. I also got involved with the self-development movement, starting with Anthony Robbins' fire-walking weekend known as 'Unleash the Power Within'. For those of you who haven't come across him, Anthony Robbins is an American success or 'peak performance' coach, 'world communicator' and 'cutting-edge, turnaround expert', and he does what he says he'll do!

I had already been surreptitiously reducing my medication, so was up for a chance to do something else to keep things under control. After an Anthony Robbins weekend, where I learned active techniques to manage my 'state' or mood, how to set and achieve goals, and, most importantly, how to look after my health, I was ready for Action!

One of the things that have made Anthony Robbins famous is that his seminars typically include participants walking barefoot across a four-metre bed of hot coals. The goal of this practice, Robbins says, is to help us realise that indeed we *can* take action and do anything we set our minds to in life. The firewalk is a metaphor for 'unlimited power'.

At midnight, having done my first fire walk, I was ecstatic. For one of the first times in my life, however, I was not 'high' and I was not 'ill'. I was experiencing positive high energy. I got home around 1 a.m., threw out my medication, and emptied my fridge and cupboards of all alcohol and unhealthy food. I started to follow Anthony Robbins' health advice rigorously. I stopped drinking alcohol, stopped eating meat, dairy produce and junk food, began exercising regularly and, apart from when I have lapsed from this regime, I have never experienced any kind of illness – mental or physical.

My friends were worried. I had changed from a fun-loving, do-anything-for-a-laugh, indulgent extremist into a teetotal, non-smoking vegetarian. No one was the slightest bit supportive of my new lifestyle choices, but that didn't matter to me. For the first time in many years, I was beginning to feel healthy – I was coming back to life. Gradually my friends accepted that this was a new phase and that I had just become a little bit weirder.

Nowadays, I work part-time in Occupational Health and General Practice, and I run a self-management focus group for people with bipolar disorder. I am not a millionaire, nor am I a charismatic leader or entrepreneur, but I am doing OK. I am mentally and physically healthier and happier than I have been in years. More importantly, I know where I am going. In 2008, I was honoured to be voted Mind's Mental Health Champion of the Year, which touched me deeply. Mind is the leading mental-health charity in the UK, and their work has touched the lives of hundreds of thousands of people. I didn't realise how many people had noticed what I was up to.

It is, therefore, my personal experiences, my work with people suffering from mental ill-health, and my medical knowledge that qualifies me to write a book like this. I remember reading John Bird's story; he created the *Big Issue*. He suggested that he was qualified to write a self-help book only because of the number of mistakes and bad decisions he has made. Equally, I feel qualified to write on MoodMapping because of the large number of opportunities that I have squandered, and the damage that I have done to myself in the process. The process of understanding this, and learning from mistakes – as well as finding solutions to the problems that undoubtedly plague many of us – has given me the tools I need to change my own life in the most positive direction imaginable, and also the lives of others.

Finding the right road

MoodMapping is a navigation system – it is your personal SatNav. I developed it to help myself, and then applied it to the lives of others as well. I've worked with people suffering from mental-health problems and mood disorders, from bipolar disease and obsessive-compulsive disorder through to PMS, postnatal illness, anxiety and plain old stress, and discovered that this system really, really works. I know it can help you, too. MoodMapping provides you with a new tool and a new way to look at your life. It is so simple and effective, it will not only change your life, but also, I hope, the lives of people around you.

Just for a minute, think how you are feeling. Now, close your eyes, and take yourself back to your last holiday where there was a lovely warm sun, beautiful sea, relaxed beach and fun meals in the evenings. Open your eyes and consider how you feel now. Even a simple imaginary exercise can change your mood, if only for a few minutes. Imagine how much better the rest of your life will be if you spend it in a good mood instead of hiding under the duvet!

How to use this book

This book is set out as a 14-day plan, which you can follow in your own way and at your own pace. Every day you'll learn a little more about yourself and your moods, and you'll acquire the tools you need both to manage them, and to experience optimum well-being. By the end of the 14 days, you'll be prepared to live your life in a different way, and interact differently with people around you.

You'll need a notebook to begin MoodMapping. Here, you'll write your notes and record your experiences. Choosing your notebook is important. It must be an object with which you feel comfortable, and perhaps even slightly celebratory, because it will eventually contain everything you need to change your life. Personally, I like hardback, lined, A4 spiral-bound notebooks, because there is plenty of room on each page, and if I make a mistake I can tear out a page without ruining the book.

After completing Days 1 to 4 of the plan, you will understand the two components of mood and the four basic mood types. You'll begin to appreciate the extent to which moods affect your thinking, your communication, what you do, how you feel and how you see the world. You will be able to map your own moods.

On Day 5, you will assess your strengths and weaknesses and come up with some strategies that will help to make anything that currently feels unmanageable a little less daunting.

Days 6 to 10 involve learning about the five key areas that affect your mood. You'll acquire some quick strategies that you can start to use to manage your moods, as well as some longer-term strategies to help get your moods under control in the coming months.

Days 11 to 14 are all about managing specific moods, such as anxiety and depression, and how to be more positive, calmer, energetic and motivated. You will also set up a plan with some medium- and long-term goals to help you live a more fulfilled and satisfying life.

Once you've got the programme underway, we'll look at more complex mood problems, such as bipolar disorder, and examine common psychological therapies and their impact on mood. And there's more! There's a section covering the way that personality and mood interact. With this knowledge, you can then move on to think about some of the broader applications for MoodMapping. For example, we'll be examining how MoodMapping can help you to interact more effectively with the people around you, and how to manage your moods in everyday life. The final chapter looks at mood disorders, which are more common than you might think.

By the end of the book, you should have identified strategies that will help you to manage your own moods and those of the people around you, and have plans in place for moving forward in your life.

Let's get started!

Day 1:
The benefits of
a good mood

Just do it!

NIKE AD

MoodMapping is a set of strategies to help you improve your mood. It may seem obvious – and certainly not a message that needs selling. But I think it does. Because having a good, healthy mood is far more beneficial than you may think, and unless you see the benefits, you may not put in sufficient hard work or have sufficient determination to take steps to improve your mood.

There is some interesting research suggesting that it takes ten thousand hours of practice to 'master' a skill, whether it be playing the violin or learning a new language. Broken down, that's about forty hours a week for five years – or perhaps about two years, if you are able to increase your mood awareness during every waking hour. I'm not suggesting that it's going to take you five years to feel the benefits of MoodMapping, but it's worth considering that making changes and becoming good at something – in this case, becoming the master of your moods – takes time, and the more practice you put in, the faster you are going to achieve it. Improvements happen gradually but you will experience benefits with each step.

The first major benefit of a good mood is that it is free! In this highly monetarised world, where even Google wants to make money from your blog, a good mood is yours for no charge. Once you have decided to change your mood, you get to choose how you feel. And the benefits of a good mood are not just a better mind, but also a healthier body.

Mood is the foundation of our mental life. It is the basis of behaviour, thinking, emotions and physical health. Bad moods give rise to bad thoughts, unhelpful emotions and poor mental and physical health, whereas a good mood gives rise to positive thinking, enhanced creativity and intelligence. MoodMapping also encourages greater self-awareness and self-knowledge, and once you know that you can *choose* how you feel, you'll feel more confident in *every* situation. This means you can always perform at your best, and will always have at your fingertips the strategies you need to change your mood, when and where you want to, in the short and long term.

With MoodMapping, you can get in the right mood or 'zone' any time you want, which gives you the freedom to make the choices you want to make at the time that is right for you.

A good mood promotes:

- **Positive health benefits.** There is now plenty of research proving that a good mood benefits physical and emotional health. A bad mood causes stress and damages our health on all levels.

- **Greater satisfaction and enjoyment.** Few people enjoy what they do while they are in a bad mood.

- **Clear thinking.** Being in a good mood makes it easier to concentrate on the important points, while being in a bad mood means you are more easily distracted, as you look for something to make you feel better.

- **Good behaviour.** Mood and behaviour go together, and with good behaviour, you can win over the world.

- **Better relationships.** It is no fun – indeed, almost impossible – to have a productive relationship with someone who is persistently in a bad mood.

- **Strong libido.** Good lovers are almost always in a good mood.

- **Solid resilience.** When you are in a good steady mood, you can be resilient and 'fake it until you make it'. You'll also have the energy to keep on trying.

- **The ability to overcome personal barriers.** It is always harder to do something when you are not in the mood. Being in a good mood improves your will-power, helps you to resist temptation, and makes doing things you don't enjoy that much easier.

- **A great sense of well-being.** You get to feel good about yourself, your future and your world. There are times when it is right to feel sad, anxious, frightened and even angry. Negative feelings can provide the push you need to start in a new direction and be more productive. Nonetheless, if negative feelings dominate your life, and you can no longer work or function normally, they are no longer healthy.

- **Physical health benefits.** People with a positive attitude recover more quickly from an injury or from surgery, and cope better with the physical symptoms of stress. A state of peace and calm has been proved to lower blood pressure and boost immunity.

- **Better management of your physical health.** Many physical illnesses are associated with depression and anxiety, including heart disease, high blood pressure, diabetes, Parkinson's disease, stroke, kidney disease, lung disease, dementia and cancer. These illnesses were rare a hundred years ago, and many were rare only thirty years ago. During this period, Western lifestyles have changed beyond recognition. The degenerative diseases of the Western world, if not immediately fatal, significantly affect our quality of life. The links between mental and physical health indicate that significant elements of these conditions relate to mental health and well-being.

- **Economic benefits.** People with a positive attitude are more likely to be promoted at work and more likely to be successful than those with a more negative approach.

MoodMapping increases your awareness of your moods, and that awareness alone can help you to manage your moods. Feeling good safeguards you from depression and anxiety and it helps to protect you from common physical illnesses. No one is too old or too young to understand themselves better. I have taught MoodMapping to teenagers and the over-sixties. I also use it on unsuspecting children to calm them down if they become too boisterous. People find it useful regardless of their age.

A healthy body is the basis of a healthy brain and mind. Mood is one way of understanding how healthy you are. By mapping your mood, you are also mapping your health. If you feel well, you probably are! And it is up to you to do your best to stay there.

A visual measure

Mood is everywhere – we always have a mood, even if we are not always aware of it. Mood is the background against which we work. It is the landscape against which our mind and body functions, and the foundation of our mental life.

On the other hand, mood is not always easy to spot. It can't be measured like blood pressure, for example. In fact, before Mood-Mapping, it was difficult to look at mood objectively, for words do not adequately describe how we feel. Words have different meanings for different people. For example, how do you differentiate between feeling annoyed and feeling irritable? There must be a difference, because there are two words; however, these are often used interchangeably, and one person will apply them differently to the next. MoodMapping provides a visual measure that avoids the linguistic subtleties of words.

Mood changes over the day. For example, you may feel better in the morning, while others don't get going until after midday. You may be a night owl, waking up in the late afternoon, peaking somewhere around midnight and lasting well into the early hours. You may be a lark, and feel fantastic from the moment you spring out of bed in the early morning. Mood can change from week to week, depending on what you are doing and where you have been. A stressful week at work will undoubtedly affect your mood, as will a holiday in the sun.

Moods affect people differently, and everyone has his or her own unique mood patterns. Some people may have relatively steady moods throughout the course of the day, which don't alter much as they travel through life. Others experience a roller-coaster of moods, and are more easily affected by what is going on around them – and inside! Others experience mood swings and changes at certain times of the day, month or even year. Our lives and our successes are defined as much by our moods as they are by our personalities.

Becoming aware

The extent to which people are aware of their moods varies. Some people are fairly conscious of changes in their moods, and how they are feeling, but not to the extent that they can manage them. Other people find it difficult to express how they feel. MoodMapping gets round the problem of putting into words how you feel, and gives you a visual tool for plotting it.

Mood awareness is a 'moment-to-moment' experience, and being aware of your mood is a way of 'living in the now'. It is a way of reconnecting with how you feel in the moment and what is happening around you. All of us spend our days adjusting the way we feel, both in the short term (by making a cup of tea, moving the position of our chair, listening to music, or ringing a friend for a feel-good chat), and in the longer term (we do this by, for example, saving for a pension to help feel more secure about the future, or planning a much-needed holiday). We go away for the weekend, decorate the house, dress up, tidy up, make a mess, go for a run, have a rest, talk to friends, spend time on our own, and find a job we enjoy.

MoodMapping provides a way to record snapshots of your mood, and offers an immediate record of how you are feeling at the moment you create your map. MoodMaps record your mood in the here and now, and they can't be used retrospectively. In other words, you can't sit down and work out how you have been feeling for the last two weeks because memories are too unreliable. For example, if your hamster died yesterday, you are more likely to report that you have felt sad for the last two weeks, rather than remember the happy day you spent with your family the weekend before. MoodMapping applies only to the moment when you make your record. Mood has to be measured in the moment. As you progress with MoodMapping, you build up a bigger picture of how your mood changes over the course of a day, a week and a month.

The key to change

Just as different keys open different locks, so it is with people. The key to one person's happiness is different to someone else's key to feeling great. For example, a night alone might create the perfect sense of happiness and relaxation for one person, while others would need an evening out to get the same effect. Some of us depend on people around us; others find happiness simply by living somewhere comfortable or using their creative talents in their work.

What's more, mood and happiness are more important to some people than to others. Some of us can get nothing done unless we are 'in the right mood'. Others can motivate themselves to get on with the job whenever they need to – perhaps because that achievement in itself is enough to make them feel good. Either way, in a good mood on a sunny day, most of us are happy to go with the flow. In a less accepting mood in the middle of winter, we are more likely to plot revolution.

Mood affects what we choose to do, how we feel and behave, how we think and how we communicate. Yet, unlike an emotion such as anger or joy, moods are not directly expressed. Rather, mood forms the background or the foundation on which different feelings and emotions grow.

The exercises

Now that you've got a basic understanding of what 'mood' is, it's time to sort out some practical applications and get started on the whole process of MoodMapping.

Many of the exercises in this book depend upon recording your mood a number of times each day, and then reflecting upon how your mood changes – across the day, over the week, and before and after specific exercises. Therefore, it's a good idea to choose certain times when you can stop whatever you are doing and record your mood. In other words, book an appointment with yourself. It's all too easy to think you'll fit it in later, and then never actually find the time. Perhaps set the alarm on your mobile phone to remind you that it's time.

😞😊 **Day 1** Exercise

Begin by opening your book. You will use a new page for each day. If your notebook is a diary, make sure there is plenty of room for each day's entry. Now, start recording your mood, three or four times a day. First thing in the morning, at lunchtime, and then in the evening are all good times. I often think it's useful to make some notes just before bedtime, when you've had a chance to re-flect upon the day a little and may be feeling calmer. If possible, stick to the same times every day, even if you are in the middle of things. Break off, record your mood, and go back to what you were doing. In this way, you'll be able to see patterns emerge.

In a couple of sentences, write down how you are feeling – are you happy, sad, anxious, or feeling satisfied? Describe your mood and, if you can, write down why you might be feeling the way that you do at that particular moment. How is your thinking? Are your thoughts coming easily or are you continually repeating the same thought? If you are feeling low, do you know what's caused you to feel that way? If you are feeling happy and calm, what has contributed to this mood?

Look back and see how your answers changed throughout the day. Consider the reasons why you may be thinking the way you do. This exercise will show you how the different aspects of what you are doing, feeling and thinking reflect your mood.

By focusing on how you feel in the moment, you become more aware of both your own mood and the moods of the people around you. This awareness is the basis upon which to manage your moods, and those of others.

When you've practised this exercise for a few days, you'll see that it can take quite a few words to describe how you feel, and that it can sometimes be difficult to find those words. It is not easy to compare how you felt at different times of the day, but it's more than likely that the mood you had in the evening was quite different to the one you experienced earlier in the day.

In the exercises for the next couple of days, you will learn how to map your moods visually and you'll see why MoodMapping is so effective. No matter how literate you are, it *is* complicated to describe how you feel, and just about impossible to draw comparisons between the feelings you have at different times of day. MoodMapping is a straightforward and quick means of describing how you feel by plotting it on a map. You can also see, at a glance, how your mood changes over the course of a day, from day to day and from week to week. What's more, it allows you to compare how you feel with how the people around you feel.

When you MoodMap, you'll be recording two elements of your mood – how much energy you have, and how good or bad you are feeling. The readings show you your mood in a way that allows you to track it over time, objectively comparing your moods from day to day, week to week, even year to year. You can also quickly see how the people around you are feeling, so that you can help manage their moods. But you should keep writing a description of your mood four times a day, as you have done in this exercise, throughout the 14 days of the plan.

Day 2:
The energy and biology of mood

Nothing is worth making
yourself ill for.

ANONYMOUS

Managing your energy effectively involves more than having enough 'get up and go'. During the day, we all have periods or waves of energy. Every one of us has a cycle of energy – perhaps lasting up to an hour – after which we need to take a short break to relax and recover. Towards the end of the working day, our energy starts to flag and it is often better at this stage to concentrate on the easier, more relaxed tasks, and to prepare ourselves to start again the following day.

You are probably already aware of whether you are a morning, afternoon or night person. However, you may not have noticed the subtle cycles and waves of energy that occur every day. By mapping your energy, you can start to see and feel how your energy changes over the day. This means you can plan your work more effectively.

Each of us has our own natural rhythm, and once you become aware of yours, you can work around it to be more productive. Equally, you can ensure that you get enough rest and variation to remain relaxed. So start thinking about what affects your energy levels throughout the day. How important are your surroundings? Do you depend on bright light to stay awake or are you naturally a night owl? Are you active? Many people are unaware that physical health and fitness play an important role in providing stamina.

Working in Occupational Health has shown me how much more alert people are when they are fit and take regular exercise. People who relax by watching TV instead of going out to engage with the world tend to be far less energetic. The benefits of exercise in protecting against depression and mental ill-health are huge.

Those around you can also affect your energy levels. Some people are livelier than others and their energy rubs off on you, while other people can be more difficult to work with. Wholesome, happy energy is a key ingredient of popularity. My friend Soames Michelson, with whom I co-founded the Doctors' Support Network, used to phone me occasionally when he felt depressed for what he called 'a touch of the manics'. I would chatter away for maybe 10 or 15 minutes. Then, suddenly, he would say, 'Thanks, that's enough', and end the call – sometimes when I was in mid-flow. He just needed a little energy boost, which was fine with me!

Being able to motivate yourself and raise your 'spirits' or energy is an important skill. Peak performance guru Anthony Robbins talks about a physical action that he calls 'Make your move'. This is a sudden, powerful gesture – perhaps punching the air, or quickly jumping – which concentrates your energy, rouses you and gets your adrenaline going. 'Making your move' gives you an instant energy boost. Because this is the UK, not America, check no one is watching you! But it's worth trying, because it is a quick and easy strategy to get your energy up instantly. If there is no one in hearing distance, shout a word that inspires you at the top of your voice – 'success', for example, or 'victory'.

Self-talk also works wonders on energy levels. For example, tell yourself how good you will feel when you have finished a task, and how excited you will be with the results. You'll be using your imagination to get some energy. I once knew a swimming coach who used to tell his charges to imagine that they were being chased by a shark to help them swim faster. Your imagination is a powerful tool, and can get you going whenever you need a boost.

Finally, some people naturally have more energy than others. One of my favourite cartoons shows a slug sitting on a stone, and the caption reads: 'I eat right, I exercise, but I still feel sluggish.' This is something we all need to take to heart. Every one of us has different types of energy.

Some people are fast, get things done quickly, and then need to rest and relax. Other people are steadier, with more stamina but less speed, and can just keep going. These people are a bit like the tortoise in the race between the tortoise and the hare. They win in the end, even if takes them longer to get there. Just as a carthorse will never win the Grand National, Desert Orchid would not be much use pulling a cart. There is no right or wrong, only what is best for different situations. If you are the slow, steady and thorough type you need to work with your natural talents, and not rush. Your energy may be just right for you. If you are fast, but not thorough, you can avoid areas that depend on slow steady progress by being aware of this.

On the other side of the equation, rest, relaxation and sleep are the opposite of 'get up and go', but are equally crucial. Good sleep is an important part of energy management, just like eating a healthy diet and getting some exercise. No one can keep going 24 hours a day without becoming stressed and exhausted. Our crazy society seems to be focused on the idea that we should always be busy – if we are awake, we should be working or out partying, or even doing the weekly shop at four o'clock in the morning. This has, and will always have, ramifications on our collective mental health, and it will affect mood more than you may think. Even the most active, energetic and happy 'do-er' needs time to recuperate. Rest, healthy living and recuperation make high, positive energy levels possible.

The biology of mood

Mood is not just 'in the mind'; it reflects the biology of the brain. How you feel is affected by the chemicals in the brain, and these are the same chemicals that form the basis of mood-altering drugs.

Within the brain there are two major systems that have an impact on mood. The Dopamine system reflects a person's arousal, or energy level. The second 'well-being' or 'housekeeping' system, the Serotonin-Endorphin system, reflects how well your organs are working, and affects how positive or well you feel. The endorphin part of the Serotonin-Endorphin system works as an internal pain-relieving system. The two parts of mood that you will chart on your MoodMap – energy and well-being – parallel these two major systems within the brain.

Dopamine, serotonin and endorphins are chemical messengers in the brain, which is made up of a tightly knit mesh of ten billion nerve cells that communicate with one another. This communication takes place through different chemical messengers or 'neurotransmitters', of which dopamine and serotonin are two of the most widely used. Other chemical messengers include GABA, acetylcholine, adrenaline, noradrenaline and endorphins. The chemical messengers pass between cells, either encouraging a nerve cell to fire off an electrical impulse, or stopping it from firing, depending on which chemical messenger is used, and where it is used.

Nerve cells outside the brain also use chemical messengers or neurotransmitters to pass on messages. They act like the electrical wiring in a house, encouraging or stopping different organs from working. Nerve cells also release chemical messengers into the bloodstream, when they become known as 'hormones'. Like neurotransmitters, hormones encourage organ function or stop organs from working when they are not needed.

Each system has many subtle inputs and adjustments to produce the enormous range of responses that even the simplest creature shows. For example, the Dopamine system helps us to respond to threats, opportunities and rewards in the environment. The Serotonin-Endorphin helps to make sure we are strong and healthy, and repairs damage. This system makes us feel good when we do something healthy, like running. Interestingly, 90 per cent of serotonin in the body is found around the gut, which may go some way to explaining the joys of comfort eating. If all else fails, head for the fridge!

The Dopamine system and Serotonin-Endorphin system work closely together, and have many connections between them. This means that a problem with one system will almost always affect the other. Nearly every major mental health problem across every age group – from autism to Alzheimer's – are linked to disturbances of either the Dopamine system or Serotonin system, or both.

The links between health, well-being, stress, energy and recovery mean that by improving your mental and physical health, you also protect yourself against the degenerative diseases of modern Western civilisation. These include heart disease, stroke, high blood pressure, stomach problems, bowel and kidney disorders. Several studies show that Alzheimer's dementia is more likely in people who drink too much alcohol, have a poor diet or are socially isolated.

Pharmaceutical companies use the biology of mood to develop drugs to treat mood disorders, such as depression and anxiety. The group of drugs, formerly known as 'major tranquillisers' and now called 'antipsychotics', block dopamine, and reduce agitation and anxiety. Although there is some overlap between the two groups of drugs, antidepressants work mainly by increasing serotonin in the brain. The purpose of this book is to show you how you can manage your own mental biology, without resorting to drugs. How can you do this? By MoodMapping, of course!

Day 2 Exercise

The next step in MoodMapping is to chart your energy level. Think of an internal scale of energy between 1 and 10. Consider 1 as feeling completely lifeless, lethargic or depressed, as if everything is too much effort. A 10 is when you are buzzing with life, vitality and high spirits. It's all go, go go!

Draw a vertical line in your notebook. Call the top of the line 10, which represents your highest energy level and the bottom of the line 1, which represents your lowest level of energy. Mark it now to represent how much energy you have at this moment.

As you write your description of how you feel at the four times of day you have selected, mark your vertical line to describe your energy level as well.

Now it's time to work out what you think may be affecting your energy level. For example, if you are feeling a bit sleepy in the afternoon, your drowsiness may relate to what you ate for lunch. What else could be at the root of your changing energy levels? Making a note now will help you to establish a pattern that will prove useful in working out the definite causes.

Over the next few days, look at the different energy levels you have recorded and see how much they vary. Although your descriptions will give you a more detailed picture of how you felt, it is easier to compare energy levels at a glance, using your vertical scale.

On the whole, if you are a morning person you will find that your energy is higher in the morning than in the evening. However, it is possible that your mark is lower on some mornings even though you tend to have more energy in the morning overall. MoodMapping provides an instant snapshot of your mood. Energy fluctuates even within the same hour, and it is possible that you recorded a morning dip with an afternoon peak, giving the appearance of having more energy in the afternoon. However, if you carry on mapping your mood over time, your records will even out and you will get a better overall picture of what your energy is like at each time of the day. That's one reason why it's important to be rigorous about mapping at the same time every day.

MoodMapping gives you an accurate impression of how your moods vary from moment to moment. Over the coming months, MoodMapping will enable you to understand yourself better and manage your mood. After a while MoodMapping becomes intuitive and you may not even need to draw it out. To begin with, however, it helps you to see your mood recorded on paper, and it can become a valuable resource as you get to know yourself and what triggers cause your mood to change.

Day 3:
Your first MoodMap

Yesterday we started mapping our energy, and today we will move on to map the other important element of mood – well-being. What's well-being? In a nutshell, it is how good or bad, or how positive or negative, you feel.

Well-being, like energy, is affected by different events in the outside world, as well as by memories or actions in your inner world. Physical health also has a significant effect on well-being, to the point where a doctor's first question is usually 'How are you feeling?' As a general rule, if someone feels well, they probably *are* well.

Humans are a social species, and we all need people – although the extent of this need varies from person to person. Some can manage well in relative isolation, while others prefer to spend their lives surrounded by others. Solitary confinement can drive you crazy but, equally, perhaps the greatest damage to our well-being is inflicted by other people, through bullying, harassment and personal attacks. In the Fire Service, I met two fire-fighters who had been bullied by the rest of their 'watch'. The 'watch' is the group of five or six men or women who live and work together for four days out of eight. The mental health of these two individuals deteriorated to the extent that they had become psychotic and required admission to hospital. Abuse damages people. Being excluded from the human tribe or, in the fire-fighters' case, excluded from the natural camaraderie of their watch, is as dangerous now as at any stage in our evolution.

Personal experience is also an important part of well-being. People who have been abused as children are more likely to suffer depression in later life. Similarly, people who experience difficulties in their marriage, or who are bullied and harassed at work, are at risk of depression. Self-esteem – how we talk to and treat ourselves – is part of well-being. People with positive self-esteem experience many personal benefits, including feeling better in themselves, and are less likely to succumb to illness than people with low self-esteem.

Finally well-being depends on being able to be yourself. People do not want to spend their lives pretending to be someone they are not. We enjoy practising our talents and want to be able to fulfil our potential at work as well as in our relationships. We all need the freedom to be ourselves and feel good about who we are. Suffocating or repressing our identities is a sure way to undermine well-being on every level.

Getting started

MoodMapping combines your energy with your well-being to give you a Moodpoint on your MoodMap. Yesterday you plotted your energy, and it's now time to plot your well-being. Your internal scale of energy is represented by a vertical line, while your internal well-being is represented by a horizontal line.

In your notebook, draw a vertical line and mark a scale on it, where 1 is at the bottom and represents the lowest energy level and 10 is at the top, representing the highest energy level. Next draw a horizontal line dissecting it and mark a scale on it, where 1 is on the left and represents the worst you have ever felt and 10 is on the right, representing the very best you have felt.

First of all, mark your energy level with a cross on the vertical line. Then think about your well-being, and how positive or negative you feel. Mark a cross on the horizontal line that best represents that point.

If you are feeling very energetic, you should have put your cross towards the top of the vertical line; if your energy level is low, your mark will be towards the bottom. If you are feeling good or happy, you should have put your mark on the right. Conversely, if you are feeling bad or unhappy, you put your mark on the left. It really is that straightforward.

For example:

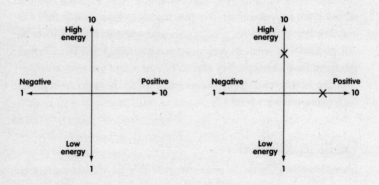

Once you have a cross on the vertical axis and the horizontal line, draw horizontal and vertical lines outwards from there and mark where the lines cross. The point at which these two lines cross shows your mood on the map.

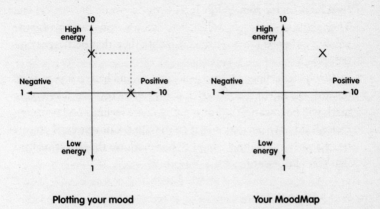

Plotting your mood   Your MoodMap

This mark represents your current mood. With a little practice, you can mark the map to chart your mood without drawing out the axes. As your energy goes up and down during the day or your sense of well-being changes, so will your mood (see below).

The higher you are on the vertical line, the more energy you have; the further to the right you are, the better you feel. Equally, the less energy you have – that is, the calmer or more exhausted you are, the lower you will be on the graph. The worse you feel, the more to the left you will be.

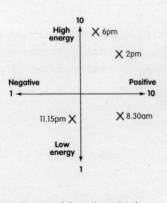

Your mood throughout the day

All of us have used maps in the past – to see where we are, and to find where we want to go. Mood-Mapping is like a road map for moods. Just as using a road map precludes long, confusing sets of verbal instructions (of the 'take a left at the end of the road, and continue over the roundabout for about two miles, past the new pub, but not as far as your old school' variety), MoodMapping allows us to plot our course visually, without scores of words and descriptions.

Moods and words

It is possible to use words to describe moods, but the meaning of a word depends not just on the exact word, but how it is used, as well as the tone of voice and intentions of the speaker. Words are, however, helpful in the process of understanding our mood, and the next exercise can help you to work out what you mean by what you say.

Mood is a form of non-verbal communication, which we share with the animal kingdom. Some experts estimate that as little as 7 per cent of communication depends on words. In practice, most communication is non-verbal. We usually know, for example, how our children feel before they tell us. Pets can rule a household without understanding many more words than 'come', 'down', 'stay' or 'no'. Lionesses hunt together with military efficiency and ants run colonies of more than a million inhabitants without a single mobile phone or computer terminal.

It is likely that we started to develop words around 300,000 years ago, and had a full language somewhere between 50,000 and 70,000 years ago. Moods and emotions account for a significant part of the way we behave towards others. Words are late arrivals on the journey of human evolution.

Language and words are contained within a small section of the brain, which is about the size of a walnut. This region is broken

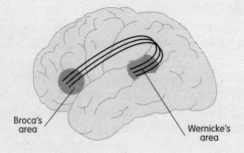

Broca's area

Wernicke's area

The speech areas in the brain

into two parts: Broca's area, which translates thoughts into words, and Wernicke's area, which translates words back into thoughts. By contrast, thinking itself seems to involve far more of the brain. People who have lost the use of language continue to function, enjoy music, make decisions and even return to work.

The function of talking takes place on one side of the brain only – on the opposite side of the brain that controls the dominant hand. So if you are right-handed, it's on your left side; if you are left-handed, it is situated on the right-hand side of your brain.

Not the only form of communication

For the many people in this world who have lost or never had the gift of speech, there is a plethora of other ways that they can communicate, and they can live full, rich lives. We depend upon speech to express ourselves but, of course, words alone are all too easily misinterpreted. And this is something that has been highlighted at a time when texts and emails form the basis of so much of the contact we have with others. Today, almost all internet chatrooms and forums, and even mobile telephones, have a ready supply of 'emoticons' as well as 'avatar' (pictures) to help us express what we want to say without words. They are now a standard feature on email and text messages. Look at the emoticons on the right; there can be no doubt that they say more than words could ever express.

Giggling

Angry

Arguing

Happy

Bravo

Crying with laughter

Feel the Heat

Grinning

Sad

MoodMaps with words

Now it's time to use words on your MoodMap, to give a name to each of the feelings you may be experiencing at the various Moodpoints. Draw a MoodMap, and write down all of the 'mood words' you can think of on your map. It may look something like the one below, but chances are you'll have your own version. You may, for example, think that 'irritated' is more negative than 'annoyed', and you may not think that 'bored' is negative at all, but, instead, closer to 'lethargic'. There is no right or wrong map; create your own.

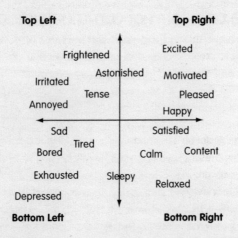

Because life is complicated, words are essential. The more complicated life becomes, the greater the vocabulary we need to describe it. Mood is the platform on which this complexity rests and until we understand our mood, it will always be difficult to be clear about the finer points of life.

Finding the right words to put a name to our mood is important, but if you struggle to define how you are feeling, the visual element of MoodMaps makes it simple to read your moods without words. It's also helpful to remember that a negative frame of mind is just your mood talking, and that you can change the message when you manage your mood.

What's your mood saying?

It becomes easier to manage your mood once you recognise that it is just your mood talking or thinking. Once your mood improves and you feel better, your thinking will improve, you will behave more positively, and you will feel better. It becomes a virtuous circle. A mood is effectively 'how you feel', and once you decide you want to change it, you have the power to do so. You can change what you do, where you are, who you are with, and how you think. This applies to any situation, whether you are suffering from exam nerves, tiredness, anger or panic attacks.

Poor moods can easily be overwhelming. In fact, the worst aspect of depression is the feeling that it will never end. However, once you accept that depression is just a poor mood – possibly representing extreme exhaustion – it becomes easier to see a way round it.

IAN

Ian is a conductor on a busy commuter route. He had been off sick with stress, following a break-up with his wife and some difficulties at work.

Once he understood his mood, and got to grips with MoodMapping, he could see why he felt the way he did and understood how he wanted to feel. He was already familiar with ways to improve his mood, including exercising and playing the guitar; however, he had not realised how important it was to work directly on his mood, and that he could manage his moods by changing the way he operated.

Once he had established this, and began regular MoodMapping, Ian started to find the motivation he needed. Within three weeks, he had found a flat on his own, which meant he could sleep undisturbed during the day when he was on a night shift. He stopped trying to contact his ex-partner, realising that she was adding to his anxiety. He talked to his manager and took a few days' annual leave to stay with his brother and his wife. He also took the opportunity to talk to his brother about what had happened to him. When I saw him again, he was a different person, having regained much of his former confidence and energy.

There were setbacks, of course. As soon as he felt better, Ian took on too much and became exhausted again. It also took him longer to recover than he thought it would. Nonetheless, within a month he was back on his feet, ready to challenge life again with his usual zest and enthusiasm.

Day 3 Exercise

This exercise is designed to show how much your mood can change in response to even the simplest exercises. Before you begin each of the exercises below, map your mood. Then, as soon as you've finished each exercise, map your mood again. See how much your mood has changed in response to different actions.

Lively music

Find a lively piece of music that you enjoy; for example, 'Walking on Sunshine' by Katrina and the Waves, or something a bit silly such as 'Nellie the Elephant'. Beethoven's *Fifth* may also do the trick. Play it as loudly as you dare and, if you can, 'dance as if no one is watching'. Do this for a few minutes, while smiling vigorously like a person deranged with happiness.

Calming music

Find a piece of music that makes you feel calm. I like Sibelius' *The Swan of Tuonela* but not everyone likes classical music, so go with something that you know makes you chill. Close your eyes and imagine you are on a warm beach, with the sea gently lapping on white sand. You are on the holiday of your dreams.

Happy memory

Think of your most important achievements over the last two or three years and choose one. Close your eyes and go back to that time. Remember how you felt, what you were thinking and doing, and how you saw the world.

Gentle breathing

Sit quietly and comfortably. Gently close your eyes and concentrate on your breathing. As you breathe out, let your body relax. As you breathe in, concentrate on the lower part of your chest. Count to one as you breathe in, and up to five as you breathe out.

Picture this

Find a picture that you like – perhaps a photograph of someone you love, or a painting that you like. Make yourself comfortable and relax in a position where you can look at the picture. Examine the whole picture – see the details, the colours it contains, and where they feature in the shot. Study the composition. Does it have people in it? Where are they? Are they in the foreground or background? What does the picture mean to you and why? Look for a few moments longer until you feel you have almost memorised what you see.

Don't forget to map your mood both before and immediately after the exercises. The change in mood that these exercises brought about may not last long. In fact, if you map your mood again about thirty minutes after you've finished an exercise, you'll probably find it's back to where it was before you began. But this does show you that it is possible to change your mood. What's more, sometimes being able to change your mood for just a few moments allows you to start a positive activity that reinforces your change in mood and makes a more permanent difference.

PAUL

Paul Jones had an exam in three weeks, and he was having trouble studying. Although he was keen to revise, he felt stress. He mapped his mood, and, not surprisingly, it showed that he was anxious. Paul's mood was 'top left'. Once he'd plotted his mood, Paul realised that he was even more stressed and anxious than he had realised, and it was preventing him from studying.

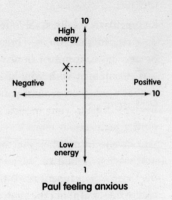

Paul feeling anxious

Paul needed to use up some of his excess energy and do something to make himself feel better. He decided he would go for a walk and listen to some of his favourite music. After half an hour, he remapped his mood and found that it had moved to 'bottom right'. He now felt calm. The walk and the music reduced Paul's anxiety. He could see this on the map, and this showed him that he was on the right path. Because he now felt calm, Paul was able to study effectively.

Reducing his anxiety had not got rid of his exam nerves, but it had made it easier for him to study. Once Paul was able to study effectively for his exams, he felt more confident. This, in turn, made him less anxious and he was able, once again, to get on with preparing for the exams ahead.

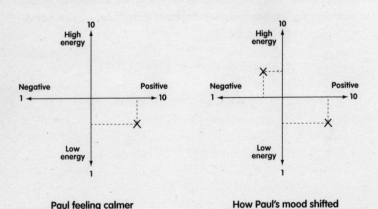

Paul feeling calmer   **How Paul's mood shifted**

Used regularly – daily, several times a day, and even hourly – Mood-Maps record how you feel. It is easier to change your mood when you are more aware of how you feel on a moment-to-moment basis. Combined with your diary, which will explain the details of what's going on around you, you'll be able to work out what might be causing your moods, and learn to identify what makes you feel better.

Continue MoodMapping three or four times a day. You will find that your mood varies, and that you start to get a picture of how your mood functions as time passes. MoodMapping isn't a quick-fix solution; in other words, it won't ensure that you always feel good. It will, however, help you to manage those days when your mood is not so good, and when that not-so-good mood is making a situation worse than it has to be.

The things that will work to change your mood will be unique to you. You may find that a holiday does the trick, or that a systematic reorganisation of your life is more helpful. You may use yoga, meditation, cognitive behaviour therapy (CBT) or exercise to alter your mood, or revert to healthy eating, regular exercise and getting enough sleep. Art, hobbies, friends and just chilling out may shift your mood. Anything goes, as long as it works for you. There is no right way to manage your mood, but there can be no doubt that the more you focus on your health and well-being, the healthier and happier you will become. Remember: good moods are healthier than bad moods.

Day 4:
The four basic moods

Before we get started, it's important to understand that moods are not emotions. We experience moods, and they are comprised of feelings; however, emotions are something quite different. They come and go, and very few of us are unaware of them. On the other hand, moods are there, all day, every day – whether we are aware of them or not.

Emotions are stronger than moods – more active and shorter lived. Even the deepest joy and greatest terror subside in minutes rather than hours. In the short term, emotions override mood but in the longer term, your mood comes back. The sudden joy of seeing someone you love can, for example, dispel your anxiety – at least in the short term. But it won't be long before the underlying depression returns. Or, look at it this way: even the worst state of panic eventually subsides in five or ten minutes, whereas a mood can last for months... and months.

Emotions are more immediate and more physical; your biology changes immediately, you grimace or break into a smile, and your breathing and heart rate reflect your growing fear or excitement. Let's say you are walking along a pleasant country path and you see a bull in the distance, charging towards you. Your reaction is immediate. A wave of adrenaline sweeps across you as you sprint for the gate. But your emotions, in this case sheer terror, fade as quickly as they arrived, even though the memory of being chased by a bull stays with you for a long time.

Things become a little complicated when we try to label emotions. For example, anxiety, fear and sadness are all words that can describe both a mood and an emotion. The difference between the two is not exact, and actually rather hard to define.

What we do know is that mood provides the soil in which emotions grow. Mood *nurtures* and *feeds* emotion. It is hard, for example, to experience a positive emotion while you are in a bad mood, and it's harder still to get angry when you are in a good mood. This is something most children understand and use to their advantage. Kids seem instinctively to read or be aware of their parents' moods, and will never choose a time when either parent is in a bad mood to drop a bombshell. Mum and Dad are much less likely to get angry about a lost blazer or a bad school report if they are in a good mood.

Neither men nor women have a monopoly on emotions and moods. Great poets and writers can be men or women. Nonetheless, different cultures have different expectations about how women and men should express themselves. Chinese culture expects women to be calm and restrained, while Middle Eastern culture expects men to express their feelings. The more fervently an Iranian man expresses his feelings, the more masculine he is considered to be. This contrasts with the 'stiff upper lip' expected of the traditional British gentleman and the emotional delicacy expected of his wife. Both men and women experience moods and emotions. However, depending on how and where they are brought up, and how their culture views the different roles of men and women, they will feel more or less able and free to express their moods and emotions.

The MoodMap divides your mood into four areas, representing the four basic moods. Even if we are unaware of *exactly* how we are feeling, it's pretty easy to work out our energy levels, and whether we are feeling good or bad.

Mood is, obviously, much more complicated than this. It's a complex mechanism, and there are certainly more than four moods; however, each of these four basic MoodMapping moods has different depths and intensities, which can, to a certain extent, be represented on the grid.

MoodMapping gives you an instant record of how you feel in the moment. By plotting your mood over time, you learn more about yourself, the extent to which your mood swings or remains stable, and how extreme or moderate it is.

Moods on the map

Let's look now at a MoodMap with the four basic moods in place. These moods are:

MOOD	LOCATION	FEELING
Action	Top Right	High energy, feeling positive
Anxiety	Top Left	High energy, feeling negative
Depressed	Bottom Left	Low energy, feeling negative
Calm	Bottom Right	Low energy, feeling positive

And here's what it looks like in practice. The four basic moods cover a lot of ground, ranging widely in strength and depth. For example, Calm can vary from intense concentration to resting in front of the television, relaxing on the beach or a deep meditative trance. Action can be energetic and productive, or it can be manic and out of control.

Mood affects your thinking, your communication, how you behave, how you feel, and how you see the world. We all know people whose behaviour varies from day to day, depending on what mood they are in. One day they are relaxed and fun to have around; the next day, if anyone

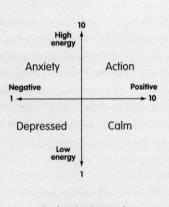

The four basic moods

speaks out of turn, there is a major storm. We also know people whose moods are as steady as a rock, regardless of what life throws at them.

Moods determine how a person behaves. For example, consider two people who are expecting a phone call from a potential date. The first person is highly anxious about dating, the second completely relaxed. The first person cancels his night out with friends in case his date phones. He continually checks his phone for messages and dares not leave the house. The second person remains relaxed, goes out with friends as planned, and puts the phone on answering machine. If the date calls, all well and good. If not, at least they didn't waste an evening waiting. The moods of each of these people has dictated the way they behaved.

Let's look at the four basic moods in detail, to get a full picture of what comprises each and how you might be feeling and behaving when you are 'in the mood'.

Action

This mood is the most popular of moods. People who have it and can spread it are popular. Just about everyone enjoys having fun, while getting on with what they need to do.

How Action thinks

In this mood, thinking is fast and electric – new ideas jump up with dramatic leaps of imagination. You make different diverse connections, seeing life as fun and positive. As the mood becomes more extreme, ideas become more exciting and more unusual. This is a confident mood, when you are ready to run and win the world. Nothing is beyond you. On the other hand, there is little time for analysis or focusing on the details, and many projects fall down without the balance of calm.

How Action communicates

In this mood you are lively and expressive, and communicate freely and passionately. You are open to new opportunities. The mood is infectious and everyone around you feels better, as you let the sunshine in. The approach is positive and dynamic. The difficulty is that if too many people come together in this mood, they may gloss over difficulties and potential pitfalls. Psychologists have called this 'group think', which is a state where individuals take their cues from each other and egg each other on, without person-ally thinking through the potential results of their actions.

This mood can be seen on the floor of the Stock Exchange, which is a high-energy environment. One moment brokers are calling 'Buy, buy, buy'. The next moment, the call is 'Sell, sell, sell', following a rumour of poor results. Fear takes over, as posi-tive energy rapidly turns negative. Common sense has long since departed, and a stock that five minutes earlier was as precious as gold dust has become worthless. Those brokers who are able to stay calm and focused, and who understand the bigger picture, are better able to ride the storms than those who are swept away by their moods.

How Action feels

This mood feels great! It is easy to mistake it for happiness. People feel as though they can conquer the world. It feels as though any-thing and everything is possible. It is the land of the impossible dream – party time. It is the mood that gets us out of bed on a dark winter morning with a spring in our step, looking forward to the new day. It is the 'can do' spirit that wins gold medals, and the mood of which we all want a taste. It is the world of rose-tinted spectacles, the cup is always half full, never half empty and life brims over with opportunity and potential.

Children are naturally in this mood, although they become dis-couraged as people tell them not to run, not to fidget, to do as they are told and not to have fun. The best days are often those that bring out the child in us.

How Action behaves

This mood is the life and soul of the party; it is the salesman who makes reluctant customers buy his whole range. It is the mood of carefree childhood – climbing trees and playing around. It over-flows with good health.

It is the mood of motivational speakers and entertainers, who can make the sun shine in the gloomiest winter afternoons. It is the mood in which leaders inspire their followers. Barack Obama is master of this state; he helps people to believe anything is pos-sible. Successful people have plenty of high-level positive energy. Margaret Thatcher was widely reported only to need four or five hours of sleep a night, and had a far greater capacity for work than anyone else in her Cabinet.

At its extremes, this mood encourages risky and impulsive be-haviours. People who are normally quite modest and restrained can, in this mood, become irresponsible daredevils, dashing from idea to idea without apparent insight or constraint.

What life looks like in Action

In this mood, you see yourself and the people around you positive-ly; the world looks full of opportunity and you have a bright fu-ture. Even people whose self-esteem is rock bottom when they are depressed feel good about themselves in this mood. Here, the worst problems are challenges or opportunities to display your skills. De-feat is not on the agenda, and every story has a happy ending!

The Action mood is fun, and although fun is an essential part of life, constant fun is not always as productive as it might be. There are times when people need to settle down to get on with their work, and reach the targets that they have set themselves in their more optimistic moments. In this mood, work may be slapdash and not as thorough as it might otherwise be. And although there is always plenty of action, those actions may not always be as well judged as they might have been had they been better planned.

Anxiety

Most of us are familiar with this mood, for even the happiest, most optimistic people can slip into anxiety. Many of us will already be aware of just what sends us there, too.

How Anxiety thinks

In this mood, it is difficult to think. The mind tends to go over the same details repeatedly, without being able to move forward. Details, rather than long-term plans and goals, become important. It is difficult to concentrate. You continually repeat the same thoughts, looking for some tiny clue that you might have missed. Two or three hours go past unnoticed. Worrying is unpleasant, but at the same time it brings a grim satisfaction. At least you are doing something, even if it is only worrying.

Once anxiety or worry has set in, it can be difficult to step back and see what is happening in a wider context. Immediate needs become all-important to an anxious person. When you are feeling anxious, your worries and concerns dominate every moment of your life, and as your anxiety spreads, even minor problems that might easily be solved assume gigantic proportions.

Anxiety eats into a person's confidence. You begin to question everything you do or say. It becomes increasingly difficult to make decisions, and you can no longer weigh the evidence objectively. Everything depends on surviving the day or the hour, whether or not it makes sense in the longer term. Worse still, every idea or potential solution is dismissed as impossible, because an anxious person immediately sees the reasons why it could not work. In this mood, thinking is pessimistic and negative.

How Anxiety communicates

Just as the thinking associated with anxiety is negative and repetitive, so is the language. Suggestions are dismissed with a resounding 'but...'. There are times when no amount of positive thinking can change the way an anxious person thinks.

When you are in an anxious state, you have to change your language. 'But' has to be one of the worst words there is in any language. It stops a conversation dead in its tracks, and demands that the listener examine all of the related potential pitfalls and negative reasoning. For example, 'I hear what you say, but I can't agree' ends all debate. It is a massive full stop. Once 'but' is in place, there is no further discussion.

How Anxiety feels

This is not a pleasant mood, nor is it healthy. It is a negative state that draws on your mental and physical reserves. Some people are better able to cope with anxiety than others. For those people who are especially sensitive to their moods, anxiety can all too easily become overwhelming. If it continues for too long, it can give rise to exhaustion and then depression, as energy and well-being run low.

All too often, you feel unable to do even simple tasks; in fact, it feels impossible to do the very things that would make you feel better. Anxiety leaves you feeling threatened and mistrustful, with low self-esteem – struggling with your work and lacking in self-confidence.

An anxious person is highly sensitive, both physically and mentally. There is a heightened awareness of your surroundings and of your physical and mental senses. Sound and other sensations become more acute; loud noises grate. Even light touch may be irritating or even painful; intense tastes become unpleasant, and every little movement makes you jump. Anxiety is not pleasant for the person experiencing it, or for the people around them. Yet people become so used to being anxious, that they assume it is normal.

How Anxiety behaves

An anxious person looks worried; eyebrows are furrowed in a frown, or raised in startled surprise with eyes staring anxiously around. You may jump at the slightest sound, pace to and fro, nervously fidget or sit motionless. You may be irritable, easily annoyed, upset or panicky, jealous or alarmed. You may want help or support one moment, and to be left alone to sort yourself out the next.

The more anxious you are, the more likely you are to become angry, panicked or paralysed by fear. Psychologists have studied the different ways that animals react to threats, and humans react in similar ways. For example, when animals are threatened they may respond by attacking furiously (in the case of a bear), or taking flight (as does a bird). A rabbit may become frozen to the spot, and a cat may hiss and bare its claws to frighten away a perceived threat. Think about it: humans are not really that different.

Fire-fighters describe how victims of a fire can become paralysed by fear to the extent that they cannot get out of their own houses or reach a fire exit. On these occasions, the ability to handle high levels of stress and anxiety can mean the difference between life and death.

Negative moods and the negative emotions associated with stress and anxiety affect both physical and mental health. Anxiety prevents you from resting, relaxing and recovering. The longer it goes on, the more likely you are to become exhausted and possibly depressed.

You may look pale and tired, and suffer from numerous physical problems, including abdominal pain and bloating, indigestion, dry mouth, palpitations, a range of aches and pains in your muscles, poor skin and posture, and muscle twitches. The long-term effects of prolonged stress and anxiety can lead to illnesses such as heart attacks, high blood pressure, stroke, cancer and other common Western diseases.

What life looks like in Anxiety

Anxiety affects the way you see the world; it erodes your self-esteem, you feel worthless, and you constantly question everything you say or do. Anxiety prevents you from trusting yourself or others, and you become suspicious of the people around you. You are constantly looking for hidden motives. Nothing is taken at face value – and that's rather like reading the small print on your pass to heaven. If something good happens, it is only because someone wants something. Cynicism and scepticism become a way of life, and nothing is what it seems. The glass is always half empty and there is no such thing as a free lunch. Nothing is certain any more. Doubt and insecurity are always present and make anxiety worse. At its extreme, anxiety becomes paranoia.

Small details become more important than the big picture. An insignificant and correctable mistake is interpreted as the whole project going wrong. Just as too much confidence means that people don't spend enough time on the details, too much anxiety can mean that they spend too long on the details. In this mood, you are reluctant to take risks, preferring to choose safety and security rather than venture into the unknown. In small doses, a healthy level of anxiety can prevent later disasters, but too much means that any new project gets bogged down in red tape, as everyone tries to make sure that nothing can possibly go wrong.

For some people, a small amount of anxiety can be a powerful motivator. You may find that you perform better because of a fear of failure. Anxiety can raise your energy. If you are about to fight a tiger or run away from a villain, you need all the energy you can get. Before a competition or big event, anxiety, if successfully managed, improves your performance. But the key word here is 'managed'.

Depressed

Depression is a mood that can be tricky, or nigh-on-impossible to evade. We describe 'sinking into depression', rather like quicksand, and that is probably a fairly accurate description. However, depression, like each of the four basic moods, can be managed and successfully overcome. The first thing you need to do is to recognise it.

How Depressed thinks

In its milder state, depressed thinking is negative and lacks imagination. It sees the reasons for not taking action, for not making any changes, and for not doing anything unnecessary. It is negative and nihilistic, with no illusions about the world. It is full of 'can'ts', 'buts' and 'if onlys'. It resents the injustice and unfairness of life.

Thinking tends to be self-obsessed, for it is difficult to take other people into account when you have no energy for anything other than your own survival. Depressed thinking cannot easily take on board new concepts, because it tends to be slow and rigid, and new ideas are sparse. It cannot plan for a future that it does not believe in; life loses its purpose and meaning, and there is no longer any reason for doing anything. Self-esteem is at rock bottom.

In its extreme, depressive thinking often includes thoughts of suicide, which may or may not be expressed. Sylvia Plath described the feeling of being separated, and experiencing no pleasure in everyday life in her novel *The Bell Jar*: 'I was so scared, as if I were being stuffed further and further into a black, airless sack with no way out.' Psychiatrists call this state 'anhedonia', or a lack of pleasure in ordinary life.

How Depressed communicates

Communication is sparse, because depression is a state of isolation. In this mood, you have little to say and rarely start a conversation spontaneously. It is a mood for thinking rather than talking. Instead of engaging with the world, you sit staring – mulling over what has happened, unable to move forward.

Like all moods, depression can affect the people around you. I know that when I have been depressed, I am not fun to be around. It can be draining to live with someone whose depression is like an emotional black hole, sucking the energy out of every encounter.

How Depressed feels

Depression, or exhaustion, is in many ways worse than anxiety. It is hard to do anything, and demands the greatest willpower to keep going. The exhaustion of depression is not the same as healthy fatigue after a job well done, which brings its own satisfaction. This is a deep malaise. Depression and exhaustion poison the mind. It is an unpleasant and potentially destructive mood.

Even the smallest activity saps what little energy you have left. It feels like wading through treacle. There is no longer any sense of time, and each day stretches on and on, unforgivingly. Everything is too much effort, too tiring, and pointless.

Depression can be mild or severe. In its milder form, it may pass within a few days, as your natural energy and resilience recovers and you can once again experience the joys of spring. Even a single good night's sleep can help you to recover from a state of depression. Depression can be due as much to emotional exhaustion as it can be to physical demands. Any new mum will identify with this, as the 24-hour demands made on her time can leave her deeply fatigued and, of course, potentially depressed.

Severe depression is difficult to describe, and unless you have experienced it personally, you may also find it difficult to understand. Once it has passed, it can be too easily forgotten, which makes it even harder to comprehend and deal with. It is not possible to 'pull yourself together' when you are depressed. It is the end of the line; every ounce of strength has been used up. If this mood did not exist, people would work themselves until they dropped. The upside of depression is that it makes people stop before they literally die of exhaustion. It is a sign of severe stress, and indicates the need for a safe place in which to recover.

Depression is a state that is largely without emotion, because emotions take energy and effort. In depression, there is no spare energy to indulge in emotional displays.

Depression may alternate with anxiety. You may become anxious and, unable to work out your anxiety, find that your problems exhaust you. This exhaustion eventually becomes depression. With the depression comes enforced inactivity. However, as soon as there are signs of recovery and energy levels start to climb again, the anxiety can return. This cycle or loop running between depression and anxiety can go for years, until something happens to resolve your anxiety or you learn to handle your depression differently.

How Depressed behaves

Depression is a low-energy, unpleasant mood. It shows in your slumped posture, lack of spontaneous movement, and lack of expression. But despite this characteristic appearance, depression all too often goes unrecognised both by you and by your family, friends and doctor.

In many ways, it can be compared to chronic physical pain, but in this case, the pain is emotional rather than physical. In extreme pain of either description, you may be frightened to move for fear of making it worse. And in both cases, pain can improve as long as you take time to relax and recover in a healthy positive atmosphere.

What life looks like in Depressed

In this mood, people see the full horror of life. There are no rose-tinted glasses that disguise problems as challenges, and challenges as opportunities. In this mood, you see everything turning out badly. You view yourself as being worthless; you feel guilty for not working harder and getting more done. You believe you are not good enough, and you find it impossible to see beyond the moment.

And, yet, there is some value in this mood, because you will have a sense of realism that precludes chasing rainbows. It is important to know that not every cloud has a silver lining.

Perhaps more than any other mood, the grim outlook of depression will help us best face up to the coming apocalypse of climate change, and other harsh realities. It is in this mood that we see life as being – in the words of the philosopher Hobbes – 'solitary, poor, nasty, brutish and short'.

Calm

The word 'calm' has intense connotations, and is almost soothing in itself. It's not surprising that this mood has a positive spin, and most of us aspire to being in a calm mood whenever we can.

How Calm thinks

Calm allows the mind to function at its best, and it encourages rational and empathic thought. This mood allows planning, decision-making and focused thinking, without being distracted by other concerns. Calm permits you to do your work thoroughly, to get to know people properly, and to make balanced judgements. It is no coincidence that the courtroom, the library and the classroom cultivate an atmosphere of calm.

Calm is the mood of reading, studying, meditating, praying, hobbies, listening to music, walking in the country and being at one with nature. It is the mood for successful negotiation, where both sides are heard equally. A calm mood helps you to plan your future, make sound decisions in the present, and learn from the past. Calm is also the mood of romance and love. Being calm and focused is about being at ease with yourself and who you are.

How Calm communicates

In counselling, there is a saying that 'You cannot argue with distress.' In other words, if you want to help someone adopt a more positive approach, it can only be done through calm discussion and active participation.

Calm communication is clear and unrushed; its aim is to be understood rather than obeyed, yet it carries with it authority. Leaders use calm to set the pace and maintain the mood. They may take their followers into action but they know always to bring them back to calm when they need to be serious.

A mother or father who can calm their child in a crisis is not only a good parent, but has also produced a child who will, when he or she grows up, know how to handle strange and potentially dangerous situations. No one can remove danger from their own or other peoples' lives, but by remaining calm, they can increase their chances of being able to work out the best course of action.

How Calm feels

Calm is all too often neglected in modern life. Calm allows you to be happy, without going crazy. It offers a deeper understanding and appreciation, and a different path to happiness than that of the Active mood.

Calm offers gentle contemplation – of nature, the kindness of friends, and the beauty of our planet. If there is any state that can be defined as happiness, or bliss, Calm must surely be it. Yet, nowadays, we too often neglect it in favour of the busy, active, stressful timetable of modern Western society.

Calm people are happy, peaceful people who make us feel good when they are around. Calmness is a mood at ease with itself and with the world. Calm is gentle and quiet; it is a place of intimacy, and a place for relaxation and healing. It is where we go when we rest, meditate, pray, and relax. It is where we get to know our friends and family at a deeper and more significant level. It is the mood where the inner voice is clear and the mind heals.

Calmness reassures the overexcited child, the angry customer and the distraught relative. Calm is a strong and assertive mood. More than depression, action or anxiety, Calm forms the platform of self-management. Being assertive is about learning to be calm in the face of authority, a bully, or any other threat.

Calm is safe. For people with mood swings or even bipolar disorder, this is the most important mood. While you are calm, you are well. Your mood is under your control, and it is a place where you are safe. It is a mood of 'being' as much as doing.

Love is the emotion of calm – and love brings well-being, peace and happiness. Love is the opposite of fear. Without love, children grow up to be anxious, fearful, insecure, neurotic, unbalanced and aggressive. Childhood love brings with it security and confidence that can last a lifetime.

How Calm behaves

Calm people are serene, their movements are unhurried, deliberate and economical. Their faces have an untroubled look, with an air of peace and stability. The sense of being is good to be around. They set their own pace regardless of what is going on around them. The calm efficiency of a well-grounded person is easily recognised.

Calmness is cool-headed and peaceful. In fact, leadership is the ability to stay calm under fire, while taking responsibility and making objective and effective decisions.

What life looks like in Calm

Calm is a mood of trust, security and faith in the future. It represents the belief that all will work out for the best in the end – and that whatever happens, it is for the best. Calm is the mood of spirituality. It seems likely that the modern West's rejection of spirituality has led to its rejection of calm. The baby has been thrown out with the bath water because calm has been the traditional comfort offered by spiritual teachers for thousands of years. Buddhism offers calm through meditation, Christianity through prayer and forgiveness.

With the loss of calm from our lives comes loss of trust, relationships, healing, health, precision and clarity. In practical terms, this means we never get a chance to catch up with ourselves or to finish what we start, especially round the home. Everyone has far too many half-finished projects, in our time-poor, materially rich society. Calm cannot be rushed; it is the first casualty in the war for ever-faster growth, and the frantic busyness of progress.

How the four moods work together

The four basic moods – Action, Anxiety, Depressed and Calm – vary in intensity and depth, and each one contributes to the creation of a fully rounded human being. Some people have a greater tendency to worry, while others seem to have limitless energy and optimism. Each mood gives rise to different experiences, and is part of being human.

😟😊 **Day 4** Exercise

We use far more 'buts' than we realise. Once you become aware of this, you'll hear it in everyone's conversation. And if the people around you are using it, chances are that you are too! Once you take the 'But' word out of your vocabulary, life begins to open up.

This exercise is about getting rid of the 'But' word, so that you can begin to find new solutions to the problems underlying any anxiety you might feel. From now on, start looking for the But word, and whenever you hear it – or hear yourself using it – quickly substitute the word 'and' instead.

For example: 'I could talk to my manager about changing my hours, but I think I am wasting my time.'

This sentence effectively ends the dialogue. Compare it with this: 'I could talk to my manager about changing my hours and I think I am wasting my time.' This leads to more, doesn't it? It suggests a continuation, which might be: 'I am looking for the right time, when he or she might be prepared to discuss it.'

When you use the word 'and', you are open to new suggestions and different ways of working.

At the beginning, you may only notice that you've used the But word after you've said it. At this stage, consciously rephrase. With practice, however, you can pick yourself up more and more quickly. Eventually you will change what you say before you've spoken the words.

Once you have taken the But word out of your own vocabulary, you can gently suggest to the people around you that they too remove it. And then step back and see how much more positive the atmosphere around you becomes.

Identifying moods

Film directors understand mood. A 250-page book can be conveyed in a 90-minute film, and in part this is because in each scene the director conveys a scene, with mood, characters and story. A film is a mood journey. A good film includes all four moods, switching from one to another, sometimes building up a mood, sometimes letting it explode onto the screen. Think of a scene from a favourite film, or the last film you saw. What was the mood? Was it action-packed with explosions, people running and high-speed car crashes, where the hero escapes against impossible odds? Did suspense build gradually, with increasing anxiety and uncertainty as it seems there is no rational way in which the hero can escape? Or was it sad, because the heroine seems doomed? Or was it perhaps a more peaceful film, where our hero looks back at what has happened to him and smiles secretly at something only you, the audience, and the hero of the film know? Films, plays and stories manage a rapid transition from scene to scene by managing the mood of their audience. Identifying the mood in different scenes in films or other TV programmes is a good way to practise Mood monitoring. You can use Mood-Mapping to document not only the overall mood of the scene but also how it changes during the scene. Does the energy increase as the scene progresses or reduce as the crisis is resolved? Does the action leave the hero feeling better or worse?

Films still require a story and characters but the action is carried forward through the changing moods of each scene. Paintings too have moods. One of the strengths of art is its ability to convey that mood to its audience and bring about a similar mood in the viewer.

From now on, whenever you watch a film or TV drama, try to be aware which of the four moods are being portrayed in each scene. You'll notice that they overlap sometimes, and that some merge naturally into others.

Identifying and understanding mood is the first step towards being able to change it.

Day 5:
Where are your strengths and what makes you anxious?

Knowing others is intelligence;
knowing yourself is true wisdom.
Mastering others is strength;
mastering yourself is true power.

TAO TE CHING

The most common reason for being unable to cope with an area of life is not because we can't do it, but because we associate it with anxiety or other negative feelings. The negative feelings or the negative mood we associate with some areas of our life can stop us from dealing with them, and this can hold us back from fulfilling our potential. If, for example, someone has difficulty dealing with money – perhaps they don't seem to manage to budget and save – then they may find they can't afford to study for the qualifications they need for their career.

There is always a reason for a mood, even if we cannot immediately work out what is causing it. We wake up 'in a mood', which gives us an idea of how the day will be, although that mood can alter throughout the day. Moods don't come out of the blue – they aren't random throws of the dice. If, for example, you wake up feeling depressed or angry, it may be because you had too much to drink the night before, or argued with a friend. Conversely, you may feel fantastic because you've had an extra hour of sleep, or you've sorted out a big project the day before.

Ignoring problems

To a certain extent, how we feel depends on what is foremost in our minds. If we think about something we enjoy, we feel better. If we spend the day working out how to afford the rent or mortgage, we will feel worse. There is a natural tendency to avoid those areas that make us feel bad, and concentrate on what we enjoy and do well. However, ignoring a problem does not make it go away. In fact, it can simmer away beneath the surface and lead to poor mood and energy levels, and can also cause your moods to become unstable.

Many of us are used to muddling through in whatever mood we might find ourselves; however, it is possible to learn to identify what is causing our moods, and then do something about it. MoodMapping is a great way to help you get there. It's worth remembering that ignoring our moods is a bit like ignoring the early warning signs at a nuclear reactor. Sooner or later there will be trouble. In order to enjoy life to the full, you have to understand your mood, understand why you feel the way you do, and know what you can do about it.

This section looks at where your strengths are and shows you the areas in which you need to pay more attention, as though you were checking the warning lights on your internal reactor.

There are any number of things that can impact on our moods, but they can be broadly categorised into five main 'keys'. Over the coming days, we'll look at these five keys, and work out how to make the changes you need in order to experience more stable, positive moods, and get the most out of your daily life.

For now, however, it's worth remembering that many poor moods, and certainly mood instability, can be caused by problems that we are not addressing. These are the difficult areas of our lives that we find tricky to handle, and they can overshadow even the most positive moods, and make us feel lousy when everything else seems to be going well. It's easy to ignore the difficult areas, and pretend that everything is going fine, or to focus on what is not going so well and become demoralised.

The importance of calm

If you experience unstable moods, or you find that your moods are sitting in the left-hand quadrants far too frequently, it's important to assess the parts of your life that may be causing problems. In my experience, almost all negative moods are missing one key element – calm. Feeling calm allows you to work towards your goals. If you are calm, you can negotiate with your mood and emotions. And, by learning calm, you learn to deal with difficult

MOOD STABILITY

An unstable mood constantly changes from minute to minute, and hour to hour. This unpredictability makes it difficult to get through the day, as even you may be unaware of how you'll respond next. When we experience unstable moods, we react erratically. So, one minute you'll be the life and soul of the party, and the next you can be impossible to live with or work for.

You can use MoodMapping to assess your mood stability. Over one day, map your mood every hour and see how much variation there is. If you find that your mood has changed significantly across the day – frequently changing quadrants – this suggests that your mood is unstable. There may be good reasons for this – for example, you may have some overwhelming problems at home or at work that are playing on your mind, or something catastrophic may have happened. You may naturally be a person whose moods fluctuate constantly, and everyone around you has come to expect this. But it is exhausting to live life this way, and it can cause your friends and work colleagues to lose patience with you, and even avoid your company.

areas. Calm allows us to achieve what we want, without being overwhelmed by anxiety. Calm is the basis of 'win win' negotiations, and confident interactions with friends and colleagues.

By dealing with areas of your life that might be causing problems, and making you anxious, and replacing your anxiety with calm, you can dramatically shift the way you feel.

By making sure that you lead a well-rounded life, you also ensure that your moods remain stable, because there will be no lurking demons on the edge of your consciousness. Ideally, there should be no area of your life that you cannot deal with. At Alcoholics Anonymous there is a saying that we are 'only as sick as our secrets', so getting yours out into the open and dealing with them can be one of the best things you can do to achieve well-being and stay well.

Calm is rational, and it helps us to see things in perspective. Many of us spend our lives in a state of anxiety or flux because we focus on imaginary threats – swine flu, paranoia about our jobs or our finances, the health of our children, or perceived threats to our relationships. Small ideas grow large in our minds because we think they are more important than they are. Those small fears then start to dominate our behaviour in ways that are unhelpful – if not downright destructive. Rather than being calm and rational, anxiety, fear, depression, paranoia and even obsession can overwhelm us and become the dominant mood we experience. So it's important to uncover the things in our lives that are making us feel this way, and then putting them into perspective, with a sense of calm.

Let me give you an example.

A visitor was entering the local mental health asylum and saw a man sitting in the corner tearing paper into tiny pieces. The visitor was curious, so he asked the man what he was doing.

'As you can see, I am tearing up paper,' said the man.

'But why are you doing that?' asked the visitor.

The man replied, 'It keeps the elephants away.'

'But there aren't any elephants in South London,' said the visitor with some confusion.

'Exactly my point,' replied the man, continuing to tear up the paper.

This man sees elephants as a threat – something that we can clearly see is false, and even ridiculous. However, he has convinced himself that his method works because there are no elephants in South London. This may sound absurd, but many of us deal with our own uniquely perceived threats in a similar way. We carry on doing things in a certain way because we think it's keeping the threat at bay. But we fail to realise that, like this man, many of our threats are imaginary. What's more, the habits and even obsessions that we develop to keep them away are destructive and undermine our moods constantly.

The problem is that it is often hard to see our own elephants. Let's look for yours now.

☹☺ **Day 5** Exercise

This exercise is designed to help you find the parts of your life that may be threatening your happiness and well-being. By identifying them, and setting them to rights, you can get on with the business of living without fear and nagging worries. You can also replace anxiety with calm, one of the most important steps you can take on the way to stable, positive moods.

Begin by making a list of the most important areas in your life. For example:

• Health

• Life partner

• Finances

• Career

• Home

• Family

• Social circle and friends

- Voluntary work

- Spirituality

- Business

- Work colleagues

- Hobbies and interests

Your list will be individual to you. Even writing out this list, however, can be enlightening. Are there whole areas of life that you are ignoring? That don't feature on your 'most important' list? Perhaps it is because you have problems here, and you are reluctant to think about them. Equally, however, you may find that one or two areas of your life are overwhelmingly central, to the point that they overshadow everything else. There may be things going on here that aren't rational, and where white elephants, or imaginary threats or concerns are lurking. The purpose of this exercise is to help you find your elephants – areas of your life that you are not dealing with effectively, and that are draining your energy and enthusiasm.

Next, draw a table with four columns. In the first column, list the various areas of your life that are important to you. Your table may look something like this:

AREA OF LIFE
HEALTH
LIFE PARTNER
FINANCIAL
CAREER
HOME
FAMILY
SOCIAL CIRCLE AND FRIENDS
VOLUNTARY WORK

SPIRITUALITY

BUSINESS

WORK COLLEAGUES

HOBBIES AND
INTERESTS

In the second column, note down how well you handle that area –
or how it makes you feel. To simplify the process, use one of four
descriptions:

• **Reasonable** (you are coping)

• **Overwhelmed** (when you are thinking about or dealing with
  this area, you find it difficult to handle, or handle it badly)

• **Suppressed** (you actively push things to do with this area to the
  back of your mind, but it is still lurking there)

• **Detached** (you've pulled away from it and refuse to
  acknowledge the problems in this area, almost regardless of
  what happens)

So, your second column may look something like this:

AREA OF LIFE	HOW I FEEL ABOUT IT
HEALTH	Reasonable
LIFE PARTNER	Reasonable
FINANCIAL	Overwhelmed
CAREER	Suppressed
HOME	Reasonable
FAMILY	Detached
SOCIAL CIRCLE AND FRIENDS	Reasonable

VOLUNTARY WORK	Reasonable
SPIRITUALITY	Overwhelmed
BUSINESS	Overwhelmed
WORK COLLEAGUES	Suppressed
HOBBIES AND INTERESTS	Detached

Once you have completed the second column, choose the six or eight most important areas in your life, and give them a score depending on how close they are to your ideal – where 10 is everything you could hope for and 0 is complete despair.

For example, you might give yourself a '2' for home. You admit you never clean, the place is always a mess, but you do remember to water your pot plants. On the other hand, you may be clean, tidy and comfortable, and give yourself an '8'.

By contrast, you may take good care of your health, eating a healthy diet, rarely drinking, and exercising regularly. So give yourself a 9.5. Your table may now look like this:

AREA OF LIFE	HOW I FEEL ABOUT IT	SCORE
HEALTH	Reasonable	9.5
LIFE PARTNER	Reasonable	10
FINANCIAL	Overwhelmed	2.5
CAREER	Suppressed	5
HOME	Reasonable	8
FAMILY	Detached	2
SOCIAL CIRCLE AND FRIENDS	Reasonable	6
VOLUNTARY WORK	Reasonable	6

SPIRITUALITY	Reasonable	8
BUSINESS	Suppressed	4
WORK COLLEAGUES	Reasonable	8
HOBBIES AND INTERESTS	Reasonable	9

Now it's time to represent each of these areas on a circle. Draw a circle in your notebook, and divide it into eight segments (or the number of areas you have listed on your table).

Label each segment with an area of your life.

Now, imagine that the outside of the circle represents a '10', and the centre a '0'. Draw a line that roughly equates to the number you've given each area of your life above. So, for example, a '5' would be about halfway from the centre of the circle to the outside rim, and a '7' would be about three-quarters of the way.

Your circle may look like this when you have finished:

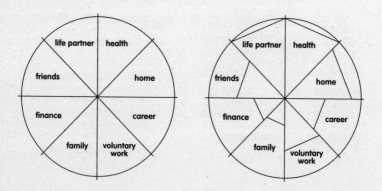

Tracing the outline, you will have a shape that looks like this:

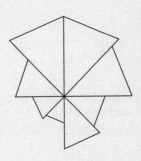

Now, if this was the wheel on your car, you'd be in for a bumpy ride. In general, people who have smooth, circular wheels cope the best with life. The more irregular yours is, the more your life needs work. You will be able to see quite clearly from this diagram where your elephants are hiding. If you've got some areas that fall well short of the rim of the circle, you can be sure they need some attention.

The simplest way to improve those areas is to start looking at what you would like to achieve in each. Then, you need to work out what you can do to make each of them a '10'. Get your notebook out again and fill in the rest of your table, heading the last column: 'What needs to happen to make this area a 10'.

Your table may look like this:

AREA OF LIFE	HOW I FEEL ABOUT IT	SCORE	WHAT NEEDS TO HAPPEN TO MAKE THIS AREA A 10?
HEALTH	Reasonable	9.5	Be more disciplined, work on improving my running
LIFE PARTNER	Reasonable	10	See what he/she needs to make it a 10 for him/her, too
FINANCIAL	Overwhelmed	2.5	Get a grip! Get some help to create workable budget; investigate different ways of making money; amalgamate debts...
CAREER	Suppressed	5	I need a way of living that makes enough money and allows me to write – investigate new job opportunities

HOME	Reasonable	8	Keep on top of the cleaning, divvy up the chores better, get some help with ironing, get dishwasher fixed
FAMILY	Detached	2	Mend relations with siblings, meet up more regularly, learn not to speak my mind, learn to say no
SOCIAL CIRCLE AND FRIENDS	Reasonable	6	Make time for old friends, return phone calls, investigate new club or group where I might meet like-minded people
VOLUNTARY WORK	Reasonable	6	Agree to regular work but with better hours, investigate options in field of interest, use writing skills?

In the areas where you've scored less than 7, go gently! If you are already anxious, don't make things worse by expecting too much of yourself, and seeing this visual model of your life as anything other than a template for making things better. Having an erratic wheel doesn't make you a bad or dysfunctional person – it simply means that your life needs a little more balance. And when you achieve that balance, you'll find that your moods follow suit.

Over the next few days, we'll look at the five keys to mood, and how they can change not only the way you feel, but the way you operate on a daily basis. Now that you know the areas of your life that need work, and have identified your own elephants, it's time to find the best ways to sort them out. Once you learn to understand your moods, and the causes for them, you can take action to improve them.

The five keys to mood are your surroundings, your physical health, your emotional intelligence (in work and relationships), what you know, and who you are (your nature). These keys also affect the way we deal with various areas of our lives. Let's start by looking at how your surroundings affect your mood.

Day 6:
Your surroundings

The world around us matters. Just about all of us would choose to stay in a luxury hotel rather than Pentonville prison. The luxury hotel would be considered a reward, while a prison cell would be a punishment. Where we live and work dramatically affects our mood, and our ability to live our lives to the full.

Used here, the term 'surroundings' describes the effect of the external physical world on our mental and physical health and well-being. From sunshine to security, from country cottage to city flat, where we live and work, and the quality of that environment, significantly affects our mood.

From an evolutionary viewpoint, our lives have always depended upon finding the right home. At one time, wild animals and marauding tribes threatened our very existence, which meant that finding the right place to live was critically important to our lives and our safety. Today, finding a nice home with a garden, within easy reach of the station, may seem a bit frivolous in comparison, but having our basic need for pleasant surroundings satisfied can be equally important in terms of our moods. The attention we pay to our housing probably harks back to the times when finding the right spot was truly a matter of life and death.

A couple of centuries ago, the Victorians understood the importance of environment on a person's physical and moral welfare. There are, for example, several 'model villages' scattered throughout England, which were built by Victorian entrepreneurs for their workforces, to be sure that they lived in acceptable conditions. Later on, the social housing of the 1950s and 1960s reflected this ideal. Nowadays, councils prefer to provide housing benefits rather than social housing, but the idea is the same – people need to have access to good-quality housing as an essential part of life.

How sensitive are you?

It has to be said that we are all different. Some people can happily live in a pigsty, and others need everything to be perfectly ordered before they feel comfortable and relaxed. Some people are acutely aware of the world around them and sensitive to the smallest nuisance. Others are almost oblivious, and just get on with their lives no matter what is going on around them.

The extent to which you are sensitive to your surroundings is an important part of your nature. Living in a rundown council block can be depressing, yet not everyone living in these blocks is depressed. While there is no doubt that most people would aspire to something better, some cope well with poor surroundings, while the surroundings of other people defines their mood and their well-being.

The power of light

Sunlight has a direct effect on the pineal gland, which is one of the parts of the brain that controls mood. Inadequate sunlight (in the winter months, for example) can lead to depression and low mood. Think about it – people are much more commonly depressed in winter than they are in summer! And it isn't just because summer brings holidays and warmer weather. So your location is important. You need to have regular access to sunshine, and not just behind a glass pane. City-dwellers may find this harder than those who live in the deepest countryside, but it is a fundamental need and something that we all have to consider. Sunshine lifts spirits in more ways than one, and directly affects mood.

Security

Another feature of emotionally healthy surroundings is security. Our homes and environments have to feel secure. Without a secure base, it is difficult to feel safe and relaxed. If your home life is not secure, it is hard to function normally. Whether that security is threatened by local vandals breaking into your house or by a difficult relationship with your partner, children or parents, the effect is the same – the foundations of your life are shaken. There is nowhere you can relax, or feel safe. It does not take much to reach the point where you are stressed and your mood is affected.

For example, there is plenty of research to suggest that children brought up in abusive environments, or who are not given a sense of security as they grow up, are at significant risk of depression later on in life. Don't underestimate how important feeling safe and secure really is.

Noise

The sounds that define your environment are also important to your well-being and your mood. Noise affects people on all levels, and there is a wealth of evidence showing that extraneous noise is stressful. As we know, stress can directly impact on mood. So whether you are living under a flight path, next to a railway or a motorway, or simply have noisy neighbours (or children!), your mood can be affected. Studies show that people do not sleep as well in noisy environments, even if they have become used to the noise and no longer notice it. In the same way, noise in your surroundings can chip away at feelings of calm, and affect your mood.

And it's not just negative 'noise' that has an impact. We know that music, perhaps more than any other single element, alters mood. Music takes its participants on a 'mood journey'. Without necessarily even using words, performers, singers, and musicians of all descriptions take their audience through a range of experiences with many different moods, whether you are listening alone to your iPod, or sharing the experience with a group of people at a concert. At the end of a great concert, the audience feels bonded together like a tribe of brothers. And that is evidence of the impact of music at its most profound. Across time, and from the earliest civil-isations, people have come together to make music, collectively lift-ing mood and forging communities with a collective spirit, through church services, concerts or other musical experiences.

The sounds you hear around you will impact on your mood positively or negatively.

What do you see?

It is not just what we hear around us that matters, but also what we see. Just as few experiences can rival waking to the dawn chorus of birds singing, waking up with a view of a riverbank teeming with wildlife is a better start to the day than seeing a canal filled with rubbish and a walkway that is unsafe after dark. Some surroundings actively lift our spirits and mood, while others drag them down.

On a smaller scale, beautiful and familiar objects can help us to feel better. Photos of family and friends, which remind us of the people we love and who love us, are important mood-lifters. Items that inspire us or encourage periods of reflection do the same.

And the colours of your environment can also play a part in your mood. A whole therapy has developed around the use of colour to manipulate mood, and there can be no doubt that it is successful. Colour actually symbolises mood. We wear black when we are mourning, and brightly coloured clothes to celebrate the joys of spring. We talk about being 'blue' or 'grey', or being 'green' with envy. Working in a bright room can cheer us up, while pastel colours work to calm. If you are perpetually angry and living in a bright red room, chances are you are feeding your anger than soothing it away with softer, healing colours like pastel green or cool blue.

At work and at play

Wherever you spend long periods of time, your surroundings will affect you. And even in the short term, a poor experience in un-healthy surroundings will impact on your mood. Many of us spend long hours at work, and these surroundings affect both our mood and our capacity for work. This premise has inspired a whole generation of interior designers and space developers, who offer to make your office brighter, lighter, and higher-ceilinged, and thus more productive and creative. Is your workplace dragging you down?

Improving your surroundings

You may already have strategies to manage your mood that involve your surroundings, and you may not even be aware that you do. For example, do you head straight to the park to sit in the sunshine during your lunch break, or take a walk in the natural world when you are feeling low? Do you watch tropical fish in a tank for a few moments, or daydream about lounging on a sandy beach with a brilliant blue sea lapping at your toes when you are feeling stressed or 'moody'? Each of these is a tool that you may unconsciously be using to improve your mood. Start paying attention to these tools, and write down in your notebook anything related to your surroundings that affects your mood.

Next, we will look at some short- and long-term strategies for improving your environment and, through that, your mood. If your 'home' wedge in the previous chapter was a little short, this section is for you! But, in fact, anyone can benefit from making their surroundings a better place to be.

Short-term strategies may not have long-lasting effects, but they can give you an instant boost, snap you out of your anxiety for long enough to get going on something that will have a longer-term impact on your mood, or even help you to concentrate. And making changes in the short term helps you to see that your moods are not 'you', but heavily influenced by something else – in this case, your surroundings.

Longer-term strategies are those that work towards a healthier you. They do not necessarily have the instant impact of a short-term strategy, and may take more effort. But they will, over time, help you to fulfil your potential, and keep your moods more balanced.

In the short term ...

Consider the following short-term measures for improving your mood by using your surroundings.

1   Focus! Find an object or picture in your environment to focus on. Just for a few minutes, look at it. If it was a gift from someone, use it to remember the good times you shared with the giver. If it is something beautiful, simply admire it. This helps you to detach from your present mood, giving you space to decide how you want to feel, and then begin finding a better and more constructive mood.

2. Tidy up! Tidying up is the quickest and easiest way to improve your surroundings. It is tiring to live in chaos, no matter how messy you may naturally be. And tidying up can be exciting! You never know what you will come across next. A tidy home or office will make you more productive and efficient, and if the Feng Shui experts are to be believed, they will also encourage a healthy flow of energy! In itself, tidying up is therapeutic.

3. Declutter, or do a little 'extreme tidying'. Everyone accumulates stuff, and stuff drags us down. Why? Because it demands attention – reminds us that we need to sort things out. Rather than being a proud symbol of our status in the world, most material goods simply represent accumulated waste. It is better to have one or two objects that you use or love, rather than diffuse your energy with shelf-loads of stuff collecting dust and draining your energy! It can be hard work, but getting rid of stuff is wonderful therapy!

4. Redecorate. Decorating makes a big difference to mood. Deliberately create a different mood in the different areas in your house, depending on what you use them for; for example, calm for the study, lively for the lounge, exotic for the bedroom and positively healthy for the kitchen. With a couple of coats of paint, you can change the colour of the walls in a day! Cover the furniture and the carpets, choose a colour and go. If you don't like the result, try again tomorrow. Use colours to represent the purpose of the room.

5. **Go somewhere different.** Take an unplanned day off, and get out and about, or at the very least visit somewhere new. Holidays help, and they needn't be expensive. As they say, 'A change is as good as a rest'. It is undoubtedly easier to relax away from the petty distractions of everyday life.

6. **Make music.** Make sure you always have a few of your favourite tracks around – whether it's CDs for the car or a play list on your iPod. In fact, why not have a play list that makes you feel cheerful and lively, and another that calms or helps you to concentrate. Don't forget to use them; the power of music is difficult to overestimate.

7. **Lighten up!** Turn on some lights to wake yourself up and turn down the lighting for a calmer, cosier mood or atmosphere. And get out in the sunshine for a natural mood-lifting experience.

8. **Say it with flowers.** Buy some flowers or, better still, pick some flowers and put them in vase. There is no quicker way to cheer up your office or your home than to place a few blooms around. You'll find yourself gazing at them, and your mood will improve.

9. **Out the window.** Look out of the window at a tree or a park; the simple sight of something natural will make you feel better.

10. **Walk in the natural world.** Get out into the countryside, or even just your local park or gardens. Studies have found that this has an immediately relaxing effect on the brain.

...And the long

These measures may be more time-consuming, but their impact on mood will be longer lasting.

1. **The right place to live.** Assess your needs and consider whether you are living in the right home for you. Are you a country person at heart who is trapped in the city? Or are you longing for the lively buzz of the city, and find the tranquil beauty of the countryside too stifling? Consider where you are in your life right now, and how you want to live. What suited you in your 20s may not be right 10 years later. Dream a little about what would suit you best, then explore the nitty-gritty details about the lifestyle that your new home would entail. If it all sounds right, maybe it's time to make a move.

2. **Renovate and redesign.** If a move is out of the question, why not make the most of the space you have now? What are you missing that you really need? What elements would enhance your life? A study? A darkroom? A library? A playroom for the kids? A kitchen with enough space to get the clutter off the worktops? Being able to control your environment is an important element of mental health, and that is the best argument for owning your own home and making it into the space you want and need.

3. **Increasing your income.** Becoming financially independent is a big enabler, and it will buy you the freedom to decide how and where you want to live. As with most things in life, financial proficiency is largely a matter of acquiring specific skills, perfecting them, and then putting them into practice. Most people can do most things, providing they have the right incentive. Sorting out your financial affairs, making sure you have enough money and a plan to reach financial freedom, is one of the foundations of good mental health. Being broke is no longer an endearing quirk. If you can get a business started in the present recession, you are on the right path.

4. **Create a garden.** This is not about calling in Ground Force and getting a team from a reality-TV show to put in an instant garden. Creating a garden is about finding a way to reconnect with the earth and with nature. You may want to grow herbs or vegetables, or simply create a place where you can feed the birds and be with nature. If a patio or a windowbox is all you have for now, make it as lush and green as you can. Use scented plants and masses of greenery to block out any surrounding concrete.

5. **Put art on your walls.** Art doesn't need to be expensive, and it can be an investment in your happiness. Smaller works by well-known artists hold their value better rather than buying something just because you like it. By comparison, there is not a lot of pleasure to be gained from looking at a share certificate!

6. **Make your own music.** Even if you never get to perform in public, being able to sing in the bath and enjoy it does wonders for your mood. Taking formal music lessons will help you to appreciate music better. Although no one would ever want to hear me play a violin, what I learnt at school means that I better appreciate those who can play well. Making music is a wonderful way to relax!

7. **Double-glaze or soundproof your bedroom.** If you have a noisy bedroom, find a way to soundproof it. This will improve your sleep enormously and, through that, your mood.

😟 😊 **Day 6** Exercise

In the back of your notebook, begin making a list of short- and long-term strategies that relate to your surroundings. Include lists of your favourite music, and how it makes you feel. For each strategy, describe when you used it, and how effective it was.

Now come up with some more. What makes you feel fantastic, and how can you incorporate it into your surroundings? Does a certain type of art relax you or fill you with contemplative awe? Maybe start your own little gallery, one picture at a time, to create a space that encourages reflection. Make a list of everything that could enhance your surroundings, and get started on finding ways to make them happen. As you do so, take time to write down when you used them, and how they made you feel.

If you scored yourself low on your home, this is an area that you may want to look at in more detail. Perhaps you hate tidying up because it was a source of family arguments when you were younger. Everyone has their own way of tidying up and sorting out their possessions. It takes time to work out where you want your things and how you would like your home to look. It also takes time to keep it tidy, but making the time can help you feel better.

People feel better for living somewhere comfortable and in a place that they feel is theirs. It may be that you don't have much confidence in your taste, but you can only find out what works for you by trying it. Don't settle for 'builders' white' because you are worried about the resale value of your house. You can always repaint when you want to move. In the meantime, this is your home – have fun!

If you scored low on your friends and social life area, once you have a home to which you are happy to invite people you will be able to entertain and make new friends. Inviting people into your home, and going to theirs, helps you to build relationships much more quickly than if you only meet at work or in coffee bars. Your home does not have to be perfect or spacious; it just needs to be welcoming and reflect who you are.

Look again at the areas where you scored yourself low, to see which ones can be improved by working on your surroundings. If you scored low on finances, would it help to have an area at home where you feel quiet and relaxed and could work on your money? Because of my academic background, I take a study for granted, and having a quiet area helps my mind focus on difficult subjects. Improving your finances means spending time studying them, and having the right environment is as important as having a calculator.

This list is the start of your own reference library of strategies to use when you need to change your mood. One of the most difficult parts of mood management is remembering to call upon strategies when you need them. Keeping them listed in your notebook will, effectively, give you your own little self-help manual and remind you that it is possible to change your mood and feel much, much better.

Next, we'll look at how your physical health affects your mood!

Day 7:
Your physical health

Health is the thing that makes you
feel that now is the best time of the
year.

FRANKLIN P. ADAMS

More than anything else, your physical health is the mood key that will determine how you feel in the long term. There is nothing better for your mood than enjoying robust good health. Good health imparts resilience, which means that regardless of what happens in your life, you can bounce back and take on the world.

It is difficult to appreciate the importance of health and energy at a time when most of us still have plenty. Some years back, wandering around a museum with my elderly parents, I remarked that I either had the time to go places or the money to go places, but never both at the same time. A retired couple, overhearing my remark, commented that there is a 'stage in life when you have both the time and the money to go where you want, but you no longer have the energy.' Being under the age of 30 at that point, I had no idea what they meant; however, as I approach their age, I understand this all too well. These days there are many opportunities for me to use the time and money that I have but, sometimes I too, lack the energy I need to make the most of them. If there is one thing that has become clear, it's the fact that energy is life.

What does this have to do with moods? When we feel down, low, depressed and lacking in energy, we cannot experience life to the full. Energy really is life – and necessary for abundant living. In many cases, we lack energy because we aren't giving our bodies the fuel they need, or treating them with the respect they deserve. Poor physical health translates into poor energy levels, and with that comes poor mood. Similarly, poor mood can affect our energy levels, so it is a double-edged sword.

However, help is at hand. Good mental health is associated with good physical health. So if you can get your physical health on course, not only will you have more energy and enthusiasm – more life – but your emotional health will improve as well. And that means your moods.

Feeling great

Many of us experience poor physical health and simply become used to feeling that way. It becomes our norm. We lack energy, sleep poorly, and become ill. It drags us down. And good physical health is much more than the absence of disease – it's about having enthusiasm for life, recovering from setbacks, and actively and energetically seeking new challenges because we have the get-up-and-go to do so.

Healthy people glow – a bit like rosy-cheeked children who've spent the afternoon in the fresh air. Unhealthy people *look* unhealthy. Their skin has a greyish tone, their movements are sluggish, and they take their time over even the smallest tasks. Not surprisingly, they are lacking in energy, and this makes them actually *appear* depressed.

And no wonder. There is much evidence showing that poor physical health is firmly linked to poor mental health, and the reverse. For example, depression is the second greatest risk factor for heart disease after smoking. After musculo-skeletal problems, mental health problems are the leading cause of ill health and absence from work. Many other illnesses are associated with anxiety and depression, and it seems that a negative mood makes illness worse, and that illness makes it harder to attain a positive mood.

Physical illness and your emotional health

Don't rule out the possibility that physical illness is affecting your moods. For example, I recently saw a young man who came to me complaining that he was depressed. I checked his five key areas, and it was clear that he lived in pleasant surroundings (in a two-bedroomed flat with his wife and young baby), his diet was reasonable, his relationship with his wife was good, and he got on well with his colleagues at work. He enjoyed his job, and was happy with his life, but he found himself inexplicably depressed.

Because there was no obvious psychological cause for his depression, I undertook a full health check and medical investigations to see if there was a physical cause for his ill health. And there was. His blood tests showed a low thyroid level, which can cause tiredness and depression. Once this was sorted out, his energy levels – and his mood – returned to normal. If you cannot find a reason for your depression or low energy in the key areas of your life, it is worth checking for physical causes. Apart from thyroid issues, they can also include low haemoglobin (anaemia) and even diabetes.

The same morning I also saw a young woman who was depressed. Again, her life seemed relatively happy; she lived with her parents, with whom she got on well. She enjoyed her job and, apart from being slightly overweight, she looked and felt well. However, it emerged that on some days she drank as many as five cans of cola. She agreed to go without for a week, drinking water or orange juice instead. When I saw her a month later, her mood had improved dramatically, and she had also lost a couple of pounds.

A can of cola contains approximately 40 grams of sugar in a concentrated phosphoric acid syrup, as well as flavourings and preservatives. Because of its high concentration of acid, as soon as cola is in the stomach, the sugar is immediately absorbed into the bloodstream. The body has to go into overdrive to find places to store the sugar in order to prevent the concentration in the blood rising to dangerous levels. The instant 'sugar rush' stimulates the brain cells but, an hour later, blood sugar levels drop right back and you feel washed out. Each can repeats the process. The continual rising and falling blood sugar affects your mood, making it unstable. It also puts your body under stress. In fact, your brain cells won't know whether they are coming or going! Drinking diet drinks does not solve the problem. Although they may not contain sugar, they contain the artificial sweetener aspartame, which has been associated with neurological and psychological effects.

Food and mood

Quite frankly, you can't have a healthy mood without a healthy diet. One of the most important things you can do when working towards stabilising and improving your mood is to look at what you eat, and how it affects you. When you choose food, instead of thinking 'What does this taste like?' you'll need to get into the habit of asking yourself 'How will this make me feel?' Because food really does impact on your mood, and pretty quickly, too.

Most of us are aware of what we *should* be eating, and what forms the basis of a healthy diet: fresh fruit and vegetables, fresh fish, meat and poultry, wholegrains, pulses, and plenty of water. Processed foods, additives and preservatives should not appear. And this type of diet leaves you energised rather than exhausted. A diet based on natural foods rarely leads to cravings or over-indulgence.

And there's more. Each of us reacts to different foods in different ways. Some of us might be sensitive to sugar. Even the natural sugars in some fruits and vegetables, can, if you are not exercising regularly or you are stressed and anxious, cause your blood sugar levels to soar and then crash, bringing with it your energy levels and your mood. That's one reason why looking at the glycaemic index (GI) count of a food may be important when you are trying to manage your moods. The higher the GI score, the more quickly your blood sugar will soar and then crash. Pure sugar is the highest GI food, and it works down from there. Low GI foods include non-starchy vegetables, lean meat and fish.

If you are sensitive to sugar you may react better to a diet based more heavily on proteins and healthy, non-animal fats, and keeping your carbohydrate intake to a minimum. Processed carbohydrates, such as cakes, biscuits and even white rice and pasta, will send anyone's blood sugar sky-high, whether they are sensitive or not. So when working to balance your moods, it's important to bear this in mind. Keep your carbs wholegrain – unrefined – and you'll partly eliminate this problem; reduce them overall, and you'll feel better still.

Caffeine is another substance that directly affects your mood. It is found in cola drinks and chocolate, not just tea and coffee. Like sugar, it can affect your energy levels by providing a burst of energy in the short term, which then dips down dramatically. If your moods are erratic, your caffeine intake may well be part of the problem.

The best foods are natural foods. If it was made in a factory and comes out of a packet, you shouldn't be eating it. A healthy diet is food that you have prepared yourself from natural ingredients. Healthy snacks are natural snacks such as a piece of fruit or some nuts or raw vegetables. Avoiding the bad stuff is generally all that is needed to bring about a dramatic improvement in your mood. The body can make what it needs, providing it has the right fuel. It is terrific at recycling! The problem is that people put the wrong fuel into their bodies, which is a bit like putting diesel into a car with a petrol engine.

Once the body has finished with a protein, it breaks it down and makes it into a new one using the parts it already has. The technical name for these protein parts are 'amino acids'. There are a small number of amino acids that the body can't make and these are called 'essential amino acids'. The body doesn't need very many of these. In fact, with a typical Western diet, our bodies are forced to spend a great deal of energy getting rid of the excess protein that we eat. As long as we don't clog the machinery with processed food, the body does an excellent job of working out what we need – and then making it from amino acids, fatty acids and carbs.

The nuts and bolts of a healthy diet

There is a large amount of contradictory information around, so it's important to apply common sense. You may have heard some of this before, but it's important to reiterate what you and your body need to ensure healthy, stable moods.

Milk and dairy: Commercial cows produce 20 litres of milk a day, and this cannot be good for you or them! To achieve this, they need massive levels of 'insulin growth hormones'. These are found in high levels in milk and have been linked with breast cancer. Even though milk is part of our culture, this does not make it good for us! Leafy green vegetables provide plenty of calcium, as do soya products, so if you get enough of them you needn't worry about cutting out milk.

Eggs: these little critters are high in cholesterol, but research seems to indicate that eating eggs doesn't necessarily affect blood cholesterol levels. Free-range eggs are a great source of protein, and they're fine to eat as part of a balanced diet.

Meat: we don't need as much of this as you may think we do. It's a good source of iron and protein, which are both important for stable moods and energy levels; however, modern, factory-farmed meat is full of saturated fat and growth hormones, as well as antibiotics and other nasties. These can affect your moods. If you do eat meat, choose wild or organic, where the same problems don't exist. Remember, too, that you can get protein from a number of other sources, including vegetables, wholegrains and pulses.

Organic food: this should feature high on your healthy-eating menu. It's usually more expensive, but it's not necessary to eat a lot. Organic fruit and vegetables not only taste better, but are grown without the use of pesticides, herbicides and chemical fertilisers. What's more they contain significantly more vitamins and minerals. So eating organic means that you are not only cutting out chemicals that could potentially make you ill, and affect your mood, but also increasing your intake of mood-boosting vitamins and minerals.

Fish oils: these have hit the headlines a lot in the last few years. Omega oils 3, 6 and 9 are essential fatty acids, which are required for good physical and mental health. The important thing is to get the balance right. We tend to get plenty of the omega 6 and 9 variety, but fall short on the omega 3s. To get what you need, make sure you eat two or three 140-gram (approximately) portions of cold-water fish, such as mackerel and salmon, every week. If you aren't a fish-eater, go for flaxseed oil. If all else fails, a supplement can help you get what you need to stabilise and lift your mood.

Water: this is an important one for a variety of reasons. First of all, drinking plenty of fresh water helps to clear the body of excess salt in our diet and waste products from body processes and food we eat. Secondly, water prevents dehydration, which can definitely affect mood and cause headaches and low energy. Drink at least a litre a day.

Snacking: eating little and often can help to keep your moods stable and your energy levels high. Not only does this ensure that your blood sugar levels are even, but it also helps prevent cravings that can lead to eating all the wrong foods. Healthy snacks such as fruits, vegetables, nuts and seeds will improve your mood, no doubt about it.

Go natural: anything that is processed, refined, full of chemicals, or high in fat, sugar and salt undermines your health. Choose your foods in their natural form, and prepare them yourself. This may require a little more work, but you'll find you have the energy and inclination to do it once your mood begins to elevate.

Avoid sugar: this gets your blood sugar soaring. While it may give you a quick 'sugar rush' and elevate your mood in the short term, you should prepare yourself for the inevitable crash. Eating natural, whole foods can help to prevent this problem, as will cutting sugar out of your diet, and choosing foods that have a low GI (see page 95).

Avoiding danger foods

We have looked at the foods that can cause problems with mood, and it's important to keep them off your menu as much as possible. When you do indulge in a bar of chocolate or a latte, remember that your mood may be negatively affected, and prepare yourself.

In a nutshell, foods that should be avoided include sugar, additives and caffeine, for the reasons listed above. Saturated fats (from animal sources), trans fats (from processed foods) and salt are also unhealthy and will impact on your overall health and, through that, your mood.

Most people in the UK drink alcohol on a regular basis but be warned that it can be one of the worst offenders in terms of your mood. For one thing, alcohol is a depressant, which means that it will leave you depressed, even if you experience feelings of happiness or euphoria at the outset. Alcohol does not just affect the brain; it affects the whole body. It can play havoc with your blood sugar, leaving you jittery, anxious and unstable. It can zap your energy. Alcohol makes mood disorders worse. Heavy drinking is associated with depression, mood swings and bipolar disorder. Once a person stops drinking, their depression improves and often disappears completely. Two-thirds of suicides are associated with alcohol, and panic disorders and anxiety disorders are commonly linked with it as well.

Alcohol first knocks out the inhibitory pathways in the brain, which are the pathways that help us to say 'no'. This gives us 'Dutch courage'. As our worries disappear, our mood is initially more cheerful. This is why alcohol is so popular at parties and special occasions. If people would leave it at an initial drink, then there would be fewer problems. However, as we consume more alcohol, it becomes harder to control our moods. Quarrels start (most violence is associated with alcohol), and thinking and physical movement are affected. And the next day? A hangover can leave you feeling worse than ever; paranoia, exhaustion, anxiety, and low energy are common features of a hangover, and have a great deal in common with unhealthy moods!

Overcoming addictions

Addictions are often the result of abusing the quick-fixes we use to change our mood and feel better, and eventually this becomes a habit. Our brains get used to the instant effects of whatever we choose to lift our moods, whether it be alcohol, prescription drugs, street drugs, tobacco, or even food. Over time, we need larger and larger 'fixes' to get the same effect, and eventually this starts to damage the brain and the body.

Learning to manage your mood without using your 'drug of choice' is the first step to overcoming addiction. Realise that you are using your 'drug' to feel better, whether you are looking for a calm mood, or the self-confidence that comes with an 'active' mood.

The first step is to be aware what you are doing to yourself, and to get to grips with the other choices you could make to manage your mood. There are many ways to change mood that do not involve using addictive drugs. By practising mood management, your brain will learn that it is not at the mercy of a chemical to bring about those changes, and MoodMapping will help to show you the way.

Getting fit

It's not just what you eat that affects your mood, either. Physical fitness works on several different levels to encourage balanced, healthy and positive moods. For one thing, it helps to ensure that you achieve good physical health, with every system and organ in the body – including the brain – working at optimum level. When you feel good physically, your mood will often follow suit. Exercise encourages the release of feel-good hormones, known as endorphins, which lift mood and act as natural pain-relievers.

The more active you are, the more alert and conscious you will be. Being physically fit gives you energy and enthusiasm. A few years ago, I worked with train drivers as an occupational health physician. Driving a train involves sitting still and concentrating for hours on end, while remaining fully alert. We found that the drivers who exercised regularly when not at work were much more alert than their sedentary colleagues.

There are three main ways to exercise and each affects mood differently:

- **Cardiovascular exercise.** This is the energetic, aerobic type of exercise that gets the blood moving around your body and the oxygen into your lungs. It includes running, swimming, brisk walking, cycling, jogging, and anything that gets your pulse rate up. This makes you fit, so you can run for a train without risking a heart attack. It's great for energy, and puts the bounce back in your step. It also works to encourage the release of endorphins, so you'll feel invigorated after cardiovascular exercise.

- **Muscle-based exercise.** This exercise is about short powerful bursts of activity, using strength rather than speed, such as lifting, digging, pulling and pushing, gardening, rugby, building work, gym weights and tug-of-war. Short bursts of activity build muscles, developing your resilience and your strength. This is great for making you feel good about yourself, especially if you are a bloke!

- **Posture exercise.** These exercises keep the body in shape and ensure that your body is being used properly. It is 'physical housekeeping' that keeps your joints in line and encourages you to use your muscles properly. This type of exercise includes yoga, Pilates, Egoscues, Alexander technique and martial arts. These exercises keep the body in shape and working efficiently. If your body is working properly, you have more energy and don't experience the pain and stiffness that come from poor posture. What's more, physical pain saps your energy and well-being, and the chemical changes in the brain associated with physical pain are the same as those associated with depression! Postural exercises are about avoiding pain and injury as much as helping you feel good. Attractive men and women have good posture.

Making exercise fun

Doing the same thing every day is boring and, just as your mind needs variety, so does your body. In order to actually get out and exercise, you'll need to find something that you enjoy – something that motivates you to get up and go. Doing it with friends is a good starting point, as you'll have fun, and be more likely to continue, because you've made a commitment. And look outside the box. Dancing is terrific exercise and will keep you fit and healthy, as well as elevating your mood. Even boxing or a game of beach volleyball or badminton will do the same. You don't have to jog around the block to get fit and experience the benefits of exercise. A cool, relaxing swim will get your heartbeat going, as will a game of football with your kids in the park. The more you do, and the greater the variety, the better you'll feel.

Up in smoke

We can't enter into any discussion about physical health without discussing smoking. Whether you are a social smoker, or a pack (or more)-a-day addict, smoking affects your mood, and on very many levels. Studies show that people who smoke report having less energy than their non-smoking peers. It also damages your skin and increases the wrinkles and that has to be depressing! Studies have shown that the reason why people find smoking addictive is because they think it makes pleasure more enjoyable and calms them down by reducing anxiety. However, anxiety levels don't actually head towards 'calm' when you smoke; instead, they fall into fatigue. And the disadvantage of these lowered energy levels is that you can't deal with the things that were making you anxious in the first place! Energy is an important part of mood that helps to keep us fit and well in the longer term.

Short-term strategies for a quick physical lift

These strategies are designed to give you a quick energy boost, which will nudge your mood in the right direction.

1. **Slow down your breathing.** Breathing is the quickest way to manage your mood. Become aware of your breathing, and slow it down if you find you have started to breathe rapidly – for example, when you become anxious. Breathing properly reduces anxiety and helps you to feel calm. The body's first reaction to feeling threatened is to increase the heart and breathing rate. By mentally controlling your breathing, you physically calm your body, and this then calms your mind. Overbreathing – in the case of panic, for example – lowers the carbon dioxide level in the blood, which chemically reduces the blood flow to the brain and other organs. This makes you feel dizzy, and stops all but the basic survival mechanisms in the brain working properly. As your panic rises, it becomes harder to make a rational decision and this increases the sense of anxiety and causes further over-breathing. By making yourself breathe calmly, you restore the balance of carbon dioxide and keep your mood under control.

2. **Get wet!** Drink water, splash it on your face, have a bath, and play with it. Water has therapeutic effects, and can help to calm and relax. Even something as simple as splashing your face with water when you feel flustered or anxious can help you to feel calm.

3. **Take a power nap.** A quick 10-minute snooze can re-energise you for the rest of the day. Close your eyes, focus on your breathing and relax your body. As you breathe out, consciously relax your muscles more with each breath. You may need to set an alarm to waken you, but with practice you can train yourself to waken after 10 minutes. Ten minutes seems to be enough to give you a quick boost, whereas if you sleep for longer, you start to enter a sleep pattern from which it is harder to wake up.

4. **Stretch!** If you are working at a desk, do some shoulder rolls. Roll your shoulders 10 times forwards and 10 times backwards, then stretch your arms out as far as you can,

trying to touch the ceiling and then the opposite walls of your office. The muscles of the neck and shoulders easily become tense, especially if you are sitting for long periods of time at a desk. When your body feels tense, this encourages you to feel anxious, because the body gives the mind the feedback that there is a crisis, and this makes the mind worry.

5. **Barefoot medicine.** Take off your socks and shoes, and walk around in your bare feet. Let your feet feel the difference between different floor surfaces, and, if the weather is nice, walk on the grass or even a sandy beach. The feet have almost as many nerve endings as your hands! Shoes stop feet feeling normal stimuli and prevent you from moving your toes around. Imagine wearing thick gloves all day and not being able to move your fingers. Tired feet make you feel tired! By giving your feet new sensations, and allowing your toes to move around, you wake up a part of your body that is normally encased in a shoe, and give yourself a quick reflexology session. And once your feet feel better, the rest of you can, too.

6. **Power move.** Invent your own Anthony Robbins-style power move, such as punching the air (see page 35), and use it!

7. **Nibble.** Have a healthy snack, a piece of fruit, or raw vegetable such as a carrot. Chew carefully and enjoy! If you have been working hard mentally, this will give a healthy energy boost. The brain uses 20 per cent of your energy, and regular snacks prevent your blood sugar from falling uncomfortably low. Chewing slowly brings out the flavours of the food, and these sensations help you feel more alert. Healthy food is energising!

Long-term strategies for optimum physical health

These strategies will help to make you healthy in the long term, and are worth considering if you want to get and stay fit and well, *and* keep your moods positive and stable. If you are physically fit and healthy, you increase your energy levels. Not only will you feel better, but you will also be able to do more of the things that make you feel good. In addition, if you are physically fit, your mind works better, which helps your self-confidence and improves your mood.

1. **Super-supplements.** The quickest and easiest way to improve your health and mood is by taking omega 3 supplements, in the form of fish oils or flaxseed. Add a good general multivitamin and mineral daily as well, as this will ensure that any trace deficiencies causing health or mood problems are addressed. Unfortunately, the food we eat is no longer as rich in nutrients as it once was, due to intensive farming methods and the fact that it tends to sit around for a while before it reaches our plates. So ensuring that you are getting everything you need by taking supplements can make all the difference.

2. **A daily dose of exercise.** Keep it fun, varied and social, which will also work to lift your mood as you get fit. Dance, play football, run, walk the dog, take the stairs rather than the lift, and run up the down escalator. The gym is fine, but keep it varied. Short bursts are fine and will all work towards physical fitness, but to experience the natural chemical lift of endorphins, it's a good idea to do something that gets your heart pumping for at least 30 minutes a day.

3. **Stand up tall.** Good posture is important. You need to aim to be balanced, so that your ears are above your shoulders, above your hips, above your knees, and above your ankles. When you sit at your desk, your shoulders, hips and knees need to be at right angles. If they are not, you can experience intense muscle tension and pain, which will make your life miserable. Chronic pain is one of the most depressing experiences you can have, as anyone with chronic arthritis will quickly tell you.

4. **Get some rays.** Sunshine is an instant pick-me-up. Just 20 minutes of midday sun, particularly in winter, will make a big difference to the way you feel. If you find the winter depressing, and can't seem to get out in the sunlight enough, consider purchasing a light box or a light visor, which will give you the rays you need. Put it on full blast while you clean your teeth and make your breakfast to ease the winter blues.

5. **Eat well.** Start the day with a homemade fresh fruit smoothie, and then continue your daily menu by focusing on natural foods. If a food was not around 10,000 years ago, then it is probably not good for you and you should not eat it. The best food is organic from your own garden or local farmer. There are many online companies selling organic vegetables, and you can have a box delivered to your door. A natural diet keeps your blood sugar steady, and that helps to keep your energy up, and aid concentration. Sugary breakfast cereals will, for example, start you off on the wrong foot in the morning. You'll experience a sugar rush, and then a fall later on in the morning, which will drag your mood with it.

6. **Bin the junk.** Treat your stomach with respect. It is one of the most complex and interesting organs in the body, with its own nervous system and 'mini-brain'. It sorts out, digests and absorbs whatever we put into it, and then gets it out into the rest of the body. Make sure you give it the right fuel. Anything that is full of chemicals, such as E numbers, preservatives, additives, colorants, and other unnatural ingredients will hamper the way your stomach does its job, and make you feel ... well, like you've eaten junk. Good, healthy food is what your body needs to feel great on all levels.

7. **No more poisons.** Alcohol and smoking need to stop, no matter how much you depend upon them. They affect every cell in the body, and undoubtedly contribute to – if not cause – mood problems.

8. **Rest and relax.** There are many ways to relax and calm the mind, from meditation and breathing exercises to repeating a mantra and even just becoming more aware of what's going on around you. Some people can relax by doing something creative, by reading, or even just napping. Everyone needs time to chill out, to rest, recover and let go of the worries of the day.

9. **Focus your mind.** In some ways this is the opposite of the last tip. Just as the mind needs to relax, it also needs to work. The most effective way to work is to focus or concentrate on one task at a time. Concentration and calm go together and people work more efficiently when they are calm. If your concentration is not good it may be because you are anxious or easily distracted. By concentrating or focusing on something outside yourself, you can reduce your anxiety, feel calmer and learn to manage your mind, so it does what you want! A healthy mind is a fit mind – one that does what you ask of it, rather than a mind distracted by every passing whim and impulse. The fitter your mind, the easier it is to get on and do what you want. This boosts your self-confidence, which makes you feel better. That, of course, improves your mood.

10. **Good-quality sleep.** The mind needs to rest and recover. Being tired or even exhausted is often a major factor in depression. If you sleep well, you are ready to face the morning, whatever it brings. Sleep problems are associated with stress and other emotional and physical problems. On average, you need about eight or eight and a half hours a night. Remember, too, that alcohol and caffeine can disrupt sleep patterns, which means that even a long sleep may not be a refreshing or rejuvenating one! The better you sleep, the better your mood, so tuck yourself up in bed with a warm drink, and shut out the world.

😠😊 **Day 7** Exercise

Now is the time to find out how much the food you eat affects your mood. You may be astonished by the results!

Over the next few days, you will be creating a 'mood and food' diary. Begin by mapping your mood before you eat. Next, write down everything you eat, and then map your mood again, about 30 minutes later. Don't forget to include the lattes and snacks you slipped in during the day!

You'll soon see how different foods affect your mood. You may also discover that you are sensitive to certain foods, such as milk products or white bread, which leave you feeling tired and perhaps a little unwell. The right foods will leave you feeling energised, and you shouldn't experience any 'dip' in your energy levels after eating them.

Make a note of the foods that seem to give you that all-important, long-term energy, and cut out, one by one, the foods that seem to drag you down, and make you feel tired and low. It will make a massive difference to the way you feel!

Day 8:
Your relationships

> The quality of your life is the
> quality of your relationships.
>
> ANTHONY ROBBINS

The support and protection that comes from good relationships are well documented. For example, one study found that single mothers are much less likely to become depressed if they have close personal relationships. Other studies have shown that people are more resilient to life's setbacks when they have good social support. Family and friends make you feel better when you are down, and put you back on your feet in a way that almost no one and nothing else can. If your family and friends believe in you, then nothing can stop you.

On the other hand, relationships that go wrong are highly damaging. Bullying and exclusion can literally drive people mad, and are some of the most traumatic experiences to endure. At home or at work, bad relationships destroy confidence, undermine health, create stress and anxiety, cause isolation, lead to withdrawal, and much, much more. When people are isolated from their community and colleagues, they are at risk of depression, poor mental health and also poor physical health.

Developing emotional intelligence

Emotional intelligence is the ability to develop and manage relationships with the people around you, with the appropriate use of verbal and non-verbal communication. It is the ability to understand and manage yourself, and to understand and manage your relationships with the people around you.

One element of this is the development of 'insight', which allows us to understand and react appropriately to the complex relationships that surround us. The first step towards insight is knowing yourself: understanding why you behave the way you do, and how you appear to others. By getting to grips with yourself, and developing some self-understanding, you'll have a great number of tools at your disposal to help you understand others

You need to consider, too, how your behaviour affects the people around you, and that means becoming a little more sensitive in your interactions. Stop and notice the impact of your words and actions. Take time to fully register the effect you are having. All too often we are tied up with ourselves and our business throughout the day, and don't stop to gauge how those around us may be affected. This is the first step towards developing insight. In fact, lack of insight is a charge frequently levelled against people who fail to understand the different ways in which people operate, or appreciate the complex nature of human interaction.

Asking people their opinions, and asking how your behaviour appears to them, is a good way to get the information you need to develop insight. The more you learn about the way other people think and feel, the more you'll understand yourself.

Basic communication

Moods are the most basic form of communication. They do not depend on words, but on instincts. People can have a good effect on your mood or a bad effect, and the closer you are to someone, the more they can affect your mood. In a trusting and supportive relationship, you grow to understand each other's moods, and can actively go about changing them for the better. We all need people to call on – people who understand us well enough to know what upsets us and what lifts our mood.

A good relationship can protect your moods, and keep them

(Continued on page 113)

RELATIONSHIP HELP:
THE FIVE KEY SKILLS OF EMOTIONAL INTELLIGENCE

I would strongly advise you to invest in a copy of one of Daniel Goleman's books about emotional intelligence, which can transform the way your relationships operate. However, it's worth looking now at a quick summary of the skills required to make your relationships emotionally intelligent, and, through that, strong enough to be satisfying and supportive to both parties. Strong relationships foster stable moods, and that's what we are aiming for.

1. **The ability to manage stress.** Stress shuts down your ability to feel, to think rationally, and to be emotionally available to another person, essentially blocking good communication until both of you feel safe enough to focus on one another. This damages the relationship. Being able to regulate stress allows you to remain emotionally available. The first step in communicating with emotional intelligence is recognising when stress levels are out of control and returning yourself and others, whenever possible, to a relaxed and energised state of awareness.

2. **The ability to recognise and manage your emotions.** Emotional exchanges are the basis of the process of communication. These exchanges are triggered by basic emotions, including anger, sadness, fear, joy and disgust, and they are also governed by moods. To communicate in a way that attracts or engages others, you have to be able to access your emotions and recognise how they influence your actions and relationships. Developing emotional awareness (being able to understand fully our motivations and needs, as well as our emotions) is the key to healthy communication.

3. **The ability to communicate non-verbally.** The most powerful forms of communication do not require words, and most take place at a faster rate than speech. Using non-verbal communication is the way to attract others' attention and keep relationships on track. Eye contact, facial expression, tone of voice, posture, gesture, touch, intensity, timing, pace and sounds that convey understanding engage the brain and influence others much more than your words alone. The signals you send will not only influence your communication within a relationship, but will also affect the collective mood.

4. **The ability to use humour and play in your relationships.** Playfulness and humour help you to navigate and rise above difficult and embarrassing issues. Mutually shared positive experiences also lift you up, help you find the inner resources needed to cope with disappointment and heartbreak, and give you the will to maintain a positive connection to your work and your loved ones. What's more, humour allows you to relax and restore energy to your relationships and everyone in them. This has the impact of lifting mood on all levels.

5. **The ability to resolve conflicts in your relationships.** The way you respond to differences and disagreements in personal and professional relationships can create hostility and irreparable rifts, or it can initiate the building of safety and trust. Your capacity to take conflict in your stride and to forgive easily is supported by your ability to manage stress, to be emotionally available, to communicate non-verbally, and to laugh easily. When conflict is resolved in a healthy way, it can be a cornerstone for trust between people. As we have seen, trust is an important element of healthy relationships and mood.

stable. In some ways, the people closest to you have a responsibility to help ensure your happiness and look out for you. They can have a dramatic effect on your moods, and that is a powerful position. Equally, however, when the people closest to you, such as your partner, your children, your friends or your boss, abuse this power, the consequences can be dreadful. There can be nothing worse for mental health than being in a relationship (any relationship) with someone who does not respect you, and whom you cannot trust. Instead of being supportive to healthy, stable moods, these types of relationship undermine mood, and eat away at your self-confidence and self-belief, which makes the situation worse. Poor relationships can make you feel stressed and anxious, and chip away at even the healthiest moods.

Developing emotional intelligence is one way to protect yourself from damaging relationships. Emotional intelligence is a science that has been studied and researched for over a decade. It can be defined as 'the inner capacity to get optimal results in relationships with ourselves and others'. According to the theories, mutual respect and effective communication are key. A primary objective is that when people interact, each person derives optimum benefit from that interaction. In many cases, relationship problems are due to a breakdown in the skills of emotional intelligence. Fortunately, it's never too late to develop these skills and raise your emotional intelligence abilities. And it follows that an emotionally healthy relationship has a much more positive impact on mood.

Difficult people

Relationships cause more problems than any other area of human activity. In many ways, given the potential difficulties, it is surprising we even talk to each other. After racism and stigmatism, perhaps one of the worst problems we face in our interactions with others is bullying. All too often, people with impressive verbal skills and high levels of social intelligence bully people who are less good at expressing themselves and are less socially capable. There are occasions when everyone is frightened of the bully, but there are also occasions when everyone, apart from the victim, thinks the bully is charming. It takes significant social skill to be able to get away with behaviour that would otherwise be considered socially unacceptable. Physical bullying is largely restricted to the playground and the criminal underworld, whereas mental bullying can happen wherever people have to work or live together.

Most people initially react to a bully by thinking that they have done something wrong – something to deserve the attack – which allows the bully to push home their advantage. Once a bully realises that he or she can get away with this kind of behaviour, it can progress to more overt bullying and harassment.

The first step to protecting yourself is to be aware that it is happening. I worked in one company where the manager appeared to be kind and thoughtful, and looking after her staff. It was not until I heard her talking to one of the staff members on the phone and accusing him of all manner of misdemeanours that it became apparent what was going on. Everyone was under a lot of pressure, but this did not excuse singling out one or two people to blame.

The next step is to draw back and understand that this is not personal. It feels personal, it looks personal and it sounds personal, but it is a reflection of the bully's personality and behaviour rather than your own. You just happen to be in the wrong place. By developing your own emotional intelligence it becomes easier to handle these people.

MoodMapping gives you an early warning system when things are going wrong. Your mood picks up difficulties long before your conscious mind is aware of them. If you can pick up a problem earlier, you can deal with it before it gets out of hand. If something doesn't 'feel right' you can start MoodMapping it, and this will help you to work out what is going on.

Short-term strategies for dealing with people

If you can get your relationships on an even keel, and interact better with those around you, your mood will follow suit. In the short term, consider the following remedies:

1. **Smile!** From small babies up to the elderly, just about everyone reacts favourably to a smile. Notice, too, that if you smile at someone they can't help but smile back – it's a natural human reaction. We all feel better if someone smiles at us, and you'll reap the rewards of the smile you receive in return. Break the ice and smile first.

2. **Random acts of kindness.** This may sound absurd, but doing something kind for someone else – no matter how small, and no matter who they are – can be uplifting. What's more, small kindnesses invite other people to return them.

3. **Little treats.** If you work in an office, bring in some flowers and put them on everyone's desks, or offer round a big box of cupcakes. Little treats or acts of generosity lift people's spirits, and the whole atmosphere improves. Try it at home, too. Leave a treat on your partner's bedside table, or your children's beds. Not only will you feel great when they respond, but they'll also know that you care.

4. **Say sorry.** Always apologise if you have done something to upset someone. Apologies clear the air. If you can't bring yourself to say sorry, you could say something along the lines of 'I am sorry you feel that way'. Most people will think you have apologised, but watch my lips!

5. **Listen!** Everyone likes an audience. People feel valued when others listen to what they say and show they have listened by responding directly. You may also learn something as well.

6. **Ask for help!** Don't hesitate to call on friends and colleagues for assistance. If you are always self-sufficient, people will begin to take you for granted. What's more, people like to help, providing they can do it reasonably easily. Showing a little vulnerability is no bad thing; no one feels close to superwoman or superman.

7. **Go easy.** Give people the benefit of the doubt. Just about everyone does the best they can with the resources they have. Trust people to do the right thing, without being naïve. A little bit of forgiveness, acceptance and gratitude goes a long way to easing human communications.

Life is made up of little moments. If you can make most of these moments good, by doing something that makes you and the people around feel better, you create a cumulative effect. Eventually, the bigger moments get better, too! People work harder and have more fun when they are in a good mood, and this impacts on relationships in every single area of your life.

Long-term strategies for better relationships

There are a number of strategies that you can employ over time to enhance your relationships with others, thus improving your overall mood. Why not consider the following:

1. **Get emotionally intelligent.** Emotional intelligence and social skills can be learned. Daniel Goleman's books allow you to test yourself to see where you fall on the scale of emotional intelligence. He's got plenty of tricks up his sleeve to help you become more 'intelligent' on the emotional front. These are well worth learning to improve your relationships, and see the positive impact on your mood.

2. **Consider counselling.** Deeper-seated relationship problems may need a little extra attention and the services of a third party. If you can't sort out your problems, they'll drag you down and impact negatively on your mood. Counselling not only clears the air, it sets out a strategy for moving forward. You'll also likely learn something about yourself and your relationships at the same time.

3. **Choose your friends carefully.** There is no point in having close relationships with people who do not respect and support you. Your friends are there to love you in good times and in bad. Being around healthy people rubs off! If you spend all your time with people who are anxious, self-absorbed and depressed, sooner or later it is going to affect you. One or two needy friends are good for the soul but, reasonably, you can only spend a part of your life helping other people. Everyone has something to offer and a balanced social network provides a wide range of friends from every walk of life. Use your calm friends to relax you, and enjoy the energy of the livelier ones. Make sure your friends are offering something to your life, and not just taking. Equally, make sure that you are enhancing theirs, too.

4. **Depend upon others.** We all depend upon others to help manage our moods and stay on an even keel. Mulling over problems on our own means that they can grow out of all proportion, and we can lose perspective. Even if we do not agree with the advice or opinions of others, their input can help us see things more clearly. And being able to shift or lighten the load a little from time to time can also help to improve mood. There is nothing like airing a problem to blow out the cobwebs and get your energy flowing again.

😣😊 Day 8 Exercise

This exercise will help you to work out how you feel about the people in your life, and whether they are lifting you up, or bringing you down.

Begin by making a list of six to ten people who have the most influence on your life – at home, at work, and in your social circle. Create two columns, writing their name in one, and their role in the other.

NAME	ROLE OF PERSON
M	Partner
J	Manager
A	Friend
SP	Aquaintance
CM	Brother
F	Father
Ch	Friend

Next, plot how they make you feel on a MoodMap by focusing on how you felt the last time you saw them. Your MoodMap may look something like this:

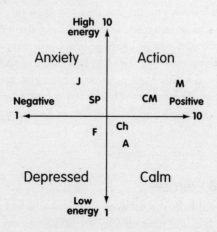

You may find that the closer you are to a person, the better they make you feel and the further their name is to the right! You may also find that you like some people more than you realised!

On the other hand, if you find that someone makes you feel bad, you need to decide whether you want to continue seeing them. If your boss makes you feel bad, you need to work out ways to improve your relationship. If your partner is putting you into a bad mood, you need to look at how you are both operating within your relationship. On the other hand, if you both help each other feel good about yourselves and each other, you are onto something!

If a friend or acquaintance makes you feel bad, chances are that you are having a similar effect on them. You need either to improve your relationship or move on. There is no benefit in having someone in your life who makes you feel bad. With this knowledge you can begin to get control of some of the relationships in your life, and understand how they affect your mood. You can also choose when to see people based on your knowledge of how they affect you, whether they are calming or energising, nurturing or requiring nurture.

Day 9:
Your knowledge

Learn from the mistakes of others.
You can't live long enough to make
them all yourself.

ELEANOR ROOSEVELT

The fourth key to mood is what you know – what you have learned to do, and what you understand, as opposed to what you do instinctively. So, you learn to play tennis or another sport, you learn to speak your language and/or another language, you learn the customs and culture of your society and you learn how to function within that society. This is your knowledge.

The way you think depends on what you know. Your knowledge is derived from anyone and anything that influences your life – your parents, schooling, friends, community, opportunities, successes and failures.

Your knowledge tells you how your world works. Because of the various experiences you have had, you have come to believe certain 'truths'. These may be influenced by your nature to some degree, but most of all they are influenced by the way you have grown to see your world. Your experiences are learned, and they define your world. If your knowledge and experiences are positive, they can build your confidence and reduce any feelings of anxiety and insecurity. Where your experiences have been negative and you do not feel sure of yourself, those beliefs and the behaviours that follow increase your anxiety and insecurity, and damage your self-esteem.

Beliefs and experiences do not just affect the relationships we have with others – they also affect the relationship we have with ourselves. For example, if you were brought up by parents who encouraged you, you start adult life with good self-esteem, believing you are a good person and capable of doing whatever you choose to do. On the other hand, if you are brought up with constant criticism, your self-esteem is likely to be poor, and you may not believe you are worthy or good enough, or capable of doing anything properly. We learn what we live, and our world is defined by that knowledge. It is what makes us what we are.

Whether we have had good or poor upbringings, there will always be areas of our lives that we find difficult – either because an experience has led us to consider it problematic, or we've learned that it is. Problem areas may make us anxious, and affect our moods. What's more, our experiences lead us to develop certain ways of thinking – both positive and negative. And it is these ways of thinking – the ways in which we use our knowledge – that most deeply affect our moods and the way we feel.

For example, you may have been terrible at maths in school. You therefore decide that you have no mathematical ability and no sense of numbers at all. You actively shy away from them, and just the thought of balancing your budget make you feel anxious. You've *learned* to feel that way through experience. That doesn't mean it's accurate or real. In fact, the maths instruction you had may have been poor, or you may have been distracted by something else during maths lesson, such as fear of a bully in the class.

In some people, the knowledge that they are no good at maths might lead to something deeper and more dangerous – it may, for example, have inspired them to believe that they are no good at *anything*. Our experiences frame our state of mind and the way we see things, and not necessarily in an accurate way.

We can, however, change the way we see things. We can relearn the way we think, and reframe our knowledge so that it enhances mood and makes us positive and energetic. We can transform negative experiences that have created negative knowledge into something positive.

ASKING POWER QUESTIONS

The human mind learns by asking and answering questions. The purpose of power questions is to remind yourself of the good things in life. If you ask questions that have negative answers, such as 'How come my kid sister gets paid more than me?' you can come up with any number of negative answers. If, however, you ask 'What have I done today that I feel good about, and has made a difference to the lives of the people around me?' you will find positive answers. Power questions give you the chance to find positive answers that leave you feeling stronger, more confident, and happier. As a result, you improve your mood.

You can gauge the impact of your 'power questions' by mapping your mood before and after asking them. So sit down with your notebook and get to work! Every day, choose one or two questions to ask yourself, and write your answers in your notebook. Take the time to map your mood, too, and you'll see the difference that power questions can make.

Ask yourself:
- What do I have to be grateful for today?
- What have I achieved today?
- What have I learnt today?
- What have I contributed today?

Your answers might be something like:
- I am grateful I remembered it was my niece's birthday before it was too late to phone!
- I am grateful for the chance to talk to my friend on the phone before she left on holiday.
- Today I managed to clear the bottom of the garden of weeds.
- Today I sent three letters that have been waiting for three weeks.
- Today I learnt how to MoodMap.
- Today I spent time learning more about the company that sends me most of my business. This will help me to pitch for more business in the future.
- Today I spoke to my friend who is having a difficult time in his relationship.

Get the idea? Take my word for it – there's always something to celebrate!

Mood and learning

We cannot learn a new skill if we are anxious or depressed. The most productive learning takes place when we are calm. If we have 'learned' to be anxious, then it is all the harder to make changes towards well-being, because we actually have to unlearn old knowledge, and replace it with new, learned knowledge.

So to move forward and alter your mood, you need to get calm. And by changing your knowledge, you'll be able to stay calm, and reframe your present and your future in a positive way.

Re-learning

Humans are naturally inquisitive people, and we acquire most knowledge by asking questions or seeking answers. The questions we ask and the answers we get decide how we consider every problem. For example, if you ask, 'Why does it always rain on my birthday?', your brain might answer 'Because I was born unlucky.' Why? Because the question almost requests a negative answer.

Richard Wiseman, who wrote *The Luck Factor*, explains that the way people think about themselves affects their luck. So, if they think they are unlucky, they will be. In order to *be* lucky, you have to *think* lucky. And you need to ask the questions that will encourage you to frame the response in a positive or 'lucky' way. So, for example, you might ask: 'Why do I never need to water my garden on my birthday?', and the answer will be a resounding, 'Because you were born lucky!'

The way you think radically affects your mood.

Reframing your knowledge

You can reframe what you know and how you use what you know. You can change the way you consider situations, and the way you see yourself. So, for example, if your house burns down, you can look for the positive. You could spend the rest of your life worrying about lost share certificates and pictures of your children, or you could consider it an opportunity to rebuild, add that second loo, add an extra storey, and contact your stockbroker to make some new investments.

Your approach depends on what you believe happened when your house went up in smoke. If you think it was the end of life as you knew and love it, you will become depressed. If you can reframe it as an opportunity, you'll find new enthusiasm. The same goes for any other experience in your life.

It's also important to overcome the 'truths' you have developed about yourself. If your experience has led you to believe that you are unlucky, hopeless, useless, slow, or any other negative thing, you will be. What you need to do is accept and see that 'truths' are not necessarily true at all – they are merely conclusions that we have drawn based on our experience. We can reframe these in almost exactly the same way that we did the experience of having a burned-down house. We can choose to focus on our good points, and actively seek them; we can look on the bright side, and actively find it. Sometimes choosing to see the bright side of life demands blind faith in the future, to believe everything will work out. But regardless of the odds, nine times out of ten that faith pays off.

More than any other species on the planet, humans depend on knowledge for survival, but that survival can be bleak or rosy, depending upon how we choose to use and frame the knowledge we have. It is not so much what we know that affects our mood, but how we interpret that knowledge. If what you know makes you feel bad, you need to look again at the way you are looking at and interpreting your experiences. If, on the other hand, you learn from your experiences (both good and bad), and appreciate that you are 'you' only because of what has happened to you, it's possible to be optimistic about your future. And being optimistic means you are in a strong, positive mood. Optimism encourages positive planning, and nudges you to take action, to take advantage of the opportunities around you. Your knowledge and the way you respond to it can most definitely influence mood to the extent that it's possible to move 'quadrants' quickly and efficiently, and to lift yourself from a bad, negative mood towards Action and Calm.

At the opposite pole, uncertainty causes more anxiety than perhaps any other single factor. When you do not know what is going to happen and when you do not know what to do, your imagination all too easily supplies the details, and this can make the unknown frightening. Once you know what is happening, know what you can do, and know what you have to do, then you can get on and do it to the best of your ability. But until you feel certain and are confident about your next step, your doubts can cause you enormous amounts of anxiety. Acquiring knowledge can provide reassurance and also choices. Making informed choices is empowering and uplifting. So use your knowledge well.

Short-term strategies to make the best use of your knowledge

The following short-term strategies are intended to help you use your knowledge to lift mood, reduce uncertainty, and create calm. Your brain works best when you are calm – and least well when you are anxious. If you manage your mood and stay calm, you can access what you know. By finding out what you already know inside, you can better work out what you need to do.

1. **Take a 'time out'.** If you find yourself in a difficult situation or awkward conversation, take time out and step back. Count to 10, breathe gently from your lower abdomen, and give yourself time for your brain to work. Deliberately slow the pace and do not start talking until you are clear what you are going to say. By taking time out, you give yourself the chance to marshal your thoughts and be clear about the points you want to make. If you can give yourself breathing space in the middle of a difficult situation, you can remember what you have done in the past, consider the various options, apply any knowledge you have to the situation, or learn something new. Whatever you do, you need space in which to do it.

2. **Use your memories.** Make a list of happy memories in your notebook. These might be linked to photographs, or cards. Keep them somewhere you can easily find them, so that if you need to remind yourself of happier times, you can do so. Remembering good times can help you to deal with less happy experiences and help protect you from becoming overwhelmed during difficult times. You will *know* you are loved, and you will know that you can be happy.

3. **Get some help.** If you have a problem, think carefully about who can help you and then call upon them. If you don't trust yourself to come up with a solution, expand your knowledge with the help of others. Get some opinions.

4. **What are your choices?** Write down at least three options in your notebook. Giving yourself a choice takes the pressure off. You probably already know what you should do but because you have not asked yourself the right questions, you can't think of the answer. Once you know what you should do, you can move forward in a positive direction.

5. **Think outside the box.** Start to ask different questions. Reframe your questions so that they demand positive answers, and consider situations from different perspectives. Ask different parts of yourself what they think. What would my responsible voice suggest? What would my frivolous, fun side suggest? What would my ethical voice say? What would my perfectionist voice say? This is another strategy to help you discover what you know. Uncertainty or not knowing what to do leads to anxiety, and this makes your mood worse. Giving yourself options and calling upon your knowledge can release you from the anxiety trap, and help you to move onwards and upwards.

6. **Sleep on it.** It may be that simple. It's amazing what our subconscious can come up with when we are asleep.

Your knowledge and the way you interpret it not only helps you to develop a positive approach to life, but also reduces the uncertainty you face, and the amount of anxiety you experience. All too often, when we find ourselves in a new situation, we are anxious; however, once you know what to do, you become confident and can develop your skills. Confidence is the antidote to anxiety!

Longer-term strategies to increase knowledge and reduce anxiety

1. **What's the worst-case scenario?** In your notebook, write down the worst that can happen – and the best. Work out how you can cope with the worst and look at ways to make the best more likely to happen. Once you know the worst that can happen, and know that you can cope with it, this knowledge helps to reduce your anxiety and enables you to do your best.

2. **Set some goals**. Be clear about what you want to achieve, then break it down into little steps. The answer to the question 'How do you eat an elephant?' ('One bite at a time') has not changed through generations of schoolchildren. Goal-setting too often leaves goals distant and out of reach, whereas the steps you need to take to reach them are equally important and need to be listed, one by one. As long as you know what you want to achieve, and know you are going in the right direction, this reduces your anxiety about what to do next. Achieving mini goals along the way to your long-term goals boosts your confidence; confidence is, without a doubt, the opposite of anxiety!

3. **Get advice.** If you feel that your life is not going in the right direction, get some advice from friends or mentors. When people do not know what to do, they feel insecure, and anxiety comes to the surface. This anxiety can stop you doing even those things that you know help. Talking to people who

have experience of your situation can help you find out what you need to do, and help you get it done.

3. **How do other people see things?** If you are in a difficult situation at work or at home, write down how other people see the situation. For example, your partner may say you are spending too much time at work, and not doing enough around the house. Your children will have an opinion, and so will your boss. Looking at everyone's perspective can help to show you ways in which you can compromise or be more flexible. In many ways this is similar to the previous strategy, which is about tapping into the knowledge around you. This knowledge helps to eradicate anxiety and provide you with confidence and certainty that you can manage in whatever situation you find yourself.

☹ ☺ **Day 9** Exercise

Look again at the areas on your circle where you scored less than 7. Now, go through the list again, and choose one area that you really want to work on. Write down what you need to *know* to get started.

For example, let's say you want to do some voluntary work with young people in your community. Start thinking about what you need to know in order to get started. You may need to find out what organisations in your area work with young people, and then make contact to find out how you can help. Once you starting learning more, you'll put the ball in action. You'll be partway to reaching your goal, which will encourage you to feel better about yourself. As a consequence, your mood will improve! When you know what you need to do, you can get started. So when you acquire knowledge, you can use it. And then it all becomes real.

Day 10:
Your nature

Be the change you want
to see in the world.

MAHATMA GANDHI

Your 'nature' is instinctive. It is who you are. As society becomes increasingly sophisticated, we become more separated from our instinctive nature. If people were computers, your 'knowledge' would be the data and software, while your 'nature' would be the computer itself. So, as a computer, you would store all kinds of data and run many different software programmes; however, regardless of how you operate and what memory you have, you will always be a Dell, an HP, a Sony, a Mac or a Toshiba. Your nature is the part of you that doesn't change – the part of you that is always you.

Your nature or your instincts are what you are born with, while your knowledge is what you acquire on the way through life. Whereas your knowledge is rational, helping you to build your skills and confidence, your nature is not rational. It depends on intuition, knowing and feeling things that you cannot always explain. It is unreasonable, and it demands that you live by your values, rather than in a way that is pragmatic and reasonable. If your spirit – the core of your nature – is crushed, it can bring on the deepest and most difficult depression. On the other hand, if your spirit (your nature) is free, you can live with passion!

Our natures are related to the way we see the world and what we value. If we are forced to conform to rules and not allowed to express our individuality, we lose the soul of our being

– both individually and collectively. A team that conforms may be obedient, but those sparks of creativity and imagination are stifled. In a nutshell, we need to express who we are in order to be true to ourselves, and live according to our values. This is a need that may, in the end, prove to be the strongest of all human needs – and perhaps the one that most affects our moods.

In the modern world, in almost every situation, knowledge over-rides instinct. It makes sense from the point of view that for civilisation to work, we have to learn to adopt a certain code of behaviour. But, to some extent, this means suppressing natural urges – repressing our instinct, or our 'nature'. This isn't a bad thing in the short term; for example, we can't all go out and thump someone if they upset us. It might be our natural urge, but we have learned and 'know' that this is not right. Over time, however, this suppression can take its toll. It can become increasingly difficult to live according to our knowledge, and keep our nature under control.

True nature will emerge

No matter what we 'know' and how well we've learned to live in society, and get on with things, there comes a time when true nature emerges. Breland & Breland were researchers who trained animals for advertisements in the 1960s. They rewarded the animals with food for doing what they wanted. They taught chickens to play football, racoons to put coins in a moneybox, and pigs to carry big circular dollars. But eventually problems occurred. After a time, and regardless of the training schedule and reward structure, the animals' behaviour returned to its natural pattern. The chickens preferred to peck the football, the racoons refused to let go of their coins, and instead of carrying them, the pigs preferred rooting around with their big circular dollars. Gradually, the animals returned to their instinctive patterns of behaviours and the training broke down.

And so it is with people. It has been said that 'You can take a lad outta Glasgow, but you canna take Glasgow outta the lad' –

and it's not just Glasgow going on here! There is something fundamental and unshiftable about our nature, and it will, over time, emerge as the strongest reckoning force. If we do not take account of this part of ourselves, and constantly try to put 'round pegs into square holes', we lose the unique spirit and meaning of what it is to be human. It goes without saying that when we lose our spirit, we lose our animating energy and our driving force. Without this, we lose hope and become depressed.

After I finally accepted my diagnosis of bipolar disorder, I lost hope that I would ever work as a doctor again. Yet, the thing that eventually made me realise that there was hope, was the understanding that I didn't need to be a doctor to help people – and that there were a hundred different ways to help people without using a stethoscope and drugs. When someone's nature or spirit is crushed, either by circumstances or the people around them, the effect on their mood can be devastating.

Achieving a balance

In order to achieve a balance, the first step is to know who you are – to understand your nature. This means knowing what is important to you, what really matters to you, and what you can't live without. These are the fundamental things – your basic needs, if you like. It's interesting that when people have survived life-changing and devastating circumstances, such as losing all of their material goods, their jobs, their houses and even their health, they often say that they've learned what is really 'important' in life. Because, in reality, the important things in life are not really what we spend the majority of our time coveting.

It is not easy to find the balance between living a life surrounded by technology, and a more natural existence that depends upon who you are, rather than which social network you belong to or the material goods you own. Part of this balance involves being true to who you are, which involves being honest, not compromising yourself and your values for the sake of more money, social status, or an easier life. It means doing what reflects your values rather than what is easiest and most convenient.

Balance also involves being tolerant of people who do not share your values, because diversity brings with it more options than conformity. This approach to life is deeply settling, and nurtures your spirit or 'nature', which underpins everything you are. As you know, this is reflected in your mood, which will blossom and soar with the right care.

Finding your values

Values are the principles on which you base your decisions, and they guide your actions. The things you value are those that are most important to you, and they become guidelines for living your life. Sometimes we find that our values have shifted through the maelstrom of daily life, and no longer represent who we are. We may also have acted or been encouraged to behave in ways that do not reflect our values – and even developed habits that are directly in opposition to them. It is, therefore, important to establish what our values are, and work out how much they mean to us. It may be time to shift our values for those that better show the people we are, and better fit our image of the people we want to be.

So be honest with yourself, and get out your notebook. Write down three events that are important to you. On my list, I would write:

• Becoming Mind Mental Health Champion 2008

• Setting up the Doctors' Support Network

• Meeting my life partner (MQ)

Then try to work out why those events are important to you. I might say that the first event was important to me because: it was a great honour; I was chosen by public vote; I was humbled by it; and, I didn't expect to win because I never win anything.

Next, try to work out what this meant to you. In my case, I felt appreciated; it was unexpected! I am always in trouble for breaking the rules. This was about being on the right side for once! When I started being open and talking and writing about my mental health problems, I did it because I was grateful for the chance I had to overcome my problems. As a doctor, I had fewer financial worries than many people, and had access to medical and scientific literature. I wanted to give something back. The award came out of the blue and it was not part of the plan. It was a wonderful surprise, and it was a boost. It also opened the door to writing this book and getting it published.

Do you get the picture?

Finally, try to summarise what the experience or event meant to you. I would probably say:

- Faith in people

- Confidence in what I was doing

- Health and healthy living

- Communication with people

- Gratitude

- Being appreciated

Do the same for the second event, and the third. By the end of the process, you will see a pattern emerging, as the same values continually appear. Put them all into list form, and then rank them in order of importance to you. You may find that there are values on your list that you don't particularly like. I did this with one man who discovered that his love of beautiful people, objects and appearances were his highest values. This was not quite the image he had of himself – but it did explain why he spent so much time looking in the mirror.

Listed in order of importance, my own final list looks like this:

- Health and healthy living
- Confidence in what I am doing
- Love
- Compassion
- Hope
- Truth
- Gratitude
- Fun
- Curiosity and understanding
- Making a difference
- Faith in people
- Communication with people
- Passion
- Companionship
- Being appreciated

Your values are the things that matter most to you – the things you can't live without. There are no 'right' or 'wrong' values, only what works best for you. As I have grown older, my values have changed, becoming simpler. In the past I thought it was over-whelmingly important to be successful in my career. I thought that by being a successful doctor I would make a difference to the lives of my patients and that it would encourage other doctors to do the same. I now realise that it doesn't matter whether I am success-ful in my career, or even whether I am a doctor. I just need to be confident that I am doing the right thing and do my best to help the people around me, accepting the limits of my inefficiency. My values are those things that I want to express in my life.

By living in a way that fits in with what you find important, you become aligned with your values. Does this give you a confident platform from which you can go full steam ahead? Why? Because you know you are going in the right direction. It's easier to be passionate about something you believe in, too, and there can be no doubt that being passionate is an important antidote to depression. It gets you up in the morning with a happy heart.

If you want to change your values to something that is closer to the real you, to your true nature, make a new list and take it with you. When you make a decision, refer to your list and use your new values to guide your choices. You can adopt your new values by using them on a daily basis. This helps you become congruent with the person you want to be and feel you are inside. The more congruent you are, the easier life gets and the better you feel. If you think it is important to help people, help them and let yourself feel good about it. A list of values reminds you what is important and reminds you of who you are inside.

Strategies to help you to understand your nature

There are some values almost everyone has. The following list gives a few examples, which you may find helpful to think about. Again, use your MoodMapping skills to see which ones work best for you.

1. **Continue to hope.** It is no accident that at the bottom of Pandora's box full of the woes of humanity was hope. Hope works in almost any situation. Hope is the light at the end of the tunnel, and it keeps people going when every logical expectation, every option, has been exhausted. Hope helps you carry on, and keeps your dreams alive. When everything else looks desperate, it helps to remember 'hope' and, with

'hope', remember your dreams. Hope stayed with me every time I was sectioned under the Mental Health Act. It did not matter what drugs the psychiatrists gave me, I never gave up the hope that one day, I would understand what was happening. I never stopped hoping that I could do something to heal the damaged people in the ward around me. Write down what you hope will happen in the next few days and weeks, and keep on hoping. Hope lifts mood.

2. **Remember what's important to you.** Whatever situation you find yourself in, it helps to ask yourself how you see the situation resolving and how you can affect the outcome. And to do this, you need to *focus* on the outcome. What is your ideal outcome – and what's important to you? In every situation, it helps to bear this in mind. From time to time I talk to doctors who have difficulties at work, or have even been suspended (often for bizarre reasons, such as forgetting to pay for a cup of coffee in the canteen). It's clear that when relationships have broken down between an employer and an employee to the point of suspension, it can be difficult for either side to work together again. So, I ask the doctor how he or she sees the situation working out. Looking at the potential outcome or end result helps the doctor see that there are options, and to work out what he or she *really* wants. A crisis often represents a chance to see what is truly important. The same goes for you, too. Look at the opportunities that await you, and bear in mind what's important to you when making your decisions. You cannot be happy if you ignore things that are important to you.

3. **Use your imagination.** If you have not got your imagination under *your* control, it is probably under someone else's. Other people use your imagination at every opportunity, rather like viruses that hijack your computer. For example, car manufacturers advertise a 4x4, showing a rugged adventurer crossing the snow-covered hillsides. This idea is ridiculously far from most people's commute to work. Nonetheless, it

appeals because it captures your imagination. You start thinking about all the ways you might use it, and before you know it, your imagination takes over and the car is yours. The car manufacturer has won. If, on the other hand, you use your imagination productively, you will be able to see new solutions to your problems, and then undertake tasks that you might normally find difficult or uncomfortable. So, if you find it difficult to talk in large groups of people, use your imagination to picture yourself talking, think through what will happen, and then reassure yourself. The great thing is that you can become confident about what you need to do without taking any risks at all. By rehearsing what you have to do in your imagination you can reduce your anxiety and help yourself feel better and be more confident.

4. **Practise positive emotions daily.** It's easy to get into a rut with your emotions. Unless you regularly practise the good ones, you won't be ready to be happy – even if you win the lottery! Every now and then we need a full emotional work-out to get things working properly. Why not spend a minute each day experiencing a positive emotion. Again, use your MoodMap to check if it helps you feel more positive. Just as a good mood helps you feel more positive emotions, by practising positive emotions you can improve your mood!

Day 10 Exercise

Every day, spend at least a little time experiencing a positive emotion. Begin by writing a list of the most positive emotions you can think of in your notebook. Choose ones that reflect your values and that you find important, then spend a minute a day concentrating on them. Take a look at the list below, if you are stuck for ideas. Just as going to the gym makes your muscles stronger, practising positive emotions makes your mind healthier. Do a quick MoodMap before you start, and again afterwards, to see if this exercise helps you feel better:

- **Gratitude.** What do you have to be grateful for? Probably lots! Grateful that you learnt to read as a child and are not struggling to learn as an adult; grateful that you have money for food and shelter; grateful that you have friends and family. Think small – be grateful that the sun is shining, or that your boss noticed your hard work. Be grateful for what you have and what you are. Meditate on gratitude for a minute or two, by thinking of everything and everyone you have to be grateful for. As you practise feeling grateful, you will find that you start to feel grateful during the day, and your gratitude will make life better and more fun.

- **Love.** Most of us take love for granted. We assume that we love our spouses, our children, our parents, our jobs and our friends. Take a minute or two just to feel that love. Think of all the people you love, one by one each day. As you practise feeling love, you will find your love becomes stronger.

- **Joy.** Many people can hardly raise a smile, let alone put the energy together to feel joyful! Spend a minute or two jumping and skipping for joy – the joy of being alive, of having woken up this morning. Celebrate the joy of a Sunday morning away from work. Have fun, for no particular reason – just because you feel like it.

- **Forgiveness.** This is perhaps the toughest emotion of all – if it is even an emotion. It means finding compassion and love for people who have hurt you. When you carry around your anger and hurt, you are the one being hurt. The process may begin by understanding what made someone behave in a way that hurt you. Sometimes people do things because they are completely unaware of the consequences of their actions. Overall, most people do the best they can, and have good reasons for behaving the way they do.

By practising positive emotions, you will find they come to the surface more easily when something good happens. This means you spend more of your time feeling good about yourself and less time feeling anxious. You feel calmer, and can be more effective. MoodMapping allows you to check regularly whether different strategies are working for you. When you find some that do, you will see your mood improve.

The five keys to mood are those areas that are most important in deciding how you feel. By nurturing each of these five areas of you and your life, you can help to ensure that your moods not only remain stable, but that they also stay positive throughout even the most difficult times. Some areas of your life may be balanced already; others may need a little work. The most important thing to remember is that when things tip out of kilter, and when your moods start to show the strain, these five areas are the place to look first. When you've established and addressed the cause of your mood problems, it's possible to see the kind of change you need, and live the kind of life you want for yourself.

Day 11:
Becoming more positive

Although the world is full of suffering,
it is also full of the overcoming of it.
HELEN KELLER

Over the first 10 days of this programme, you've learnt how to MoodMap, and discovered how the various parts of your life – and, indeed, you – can influence your mood. You've also learnt some strategies to help change your mood. Over the next 4 days, we'll get to work on improving your mood – specially if you spend a lot of time on the left-hand side of your MoodMap.

The next 4 days target major mood shifts from Anxiety and Depression to Action and Calm. Moods can be as much a habit as a response to what is happening to you directly. These days will challenge how you feel, and show you ways to change it.

Old habits die hard

Old habits feel comfortable. It takes an effort to make changes and most people lead full lives without spare time or energy. It sometimes seems impossible to do things differently, because change means adapting habits, and acting habitually is quicker and easier.

Successful change depends on understanding what you need to do, believing it is important, knowing you can do it and being determined to succeed. Change takes energy, time and effort. There is no easy way. It is not surprising that most people only change when they have no other choice.

This was true for me. I had reached the point where I was prepared to do just about anything to avoid being ill again. I was married, I had a comfortable life, and was doing more or less what I wanted, but I was still taking medication and there were many things I could not do because of my 'illness'. I was also increasingly frightened by the prospect of being ill again. My psychiatrist told me it was only a matter of time before my next episode of severe depression or hypomania, and my family and friends were certain I would never work again. I was desperate to sort out my bipolar mood disorder. Once I reached the point of 'never again!' it became possible to change my life.

Two ways to change

The first way to make changes is to take a dramatic step, deciding in a moment that you will no longer tolerate what has happened in the past. You have decided that enough is enough. Sometimes this impetus creates the most profound change, because you have developed a steely determination that will see you through the process.

The second way is gentler, and consists of a series of little steps. You know what you should do, and you know you have to change. However, instead of doing everything at once, you do it a little bit at a time. By taking one step at a time, you gradually change direction without pushing yourself too hard, and you make sure you succeed in each stage. As you keep making positive changes in your life, you find yourself in a happier, healthier place.

How does this apply to mood? In the first instance, it's important to remember that all moods have a cause. If you change the root cause, then your mood will follow suit. Furthermore, mood is a choice. It may not be a completely free choice, but you can choose which of the four moods you spend the most time in.

Mood-management is a skill that you can learn, and it improves with practice. It takes insight, discipline and repetition to become a finely honed skill.

Using MoodMapping to change your mood

MoodMapping helps you understand how you react to events and what makes you feel the way you do. You may have found that simply becoming more aware of your moods has led to some improvement! Over the next few days we'll look at how to make major changes to your mood. A poor mood distorts your thinking, and makes you behave in ways that you later regret. You'll also miss opportunities, and perhaps even lose friends.

For each mood shift, we'll look at various strategies, which are grouped according to the 5 keys to mood. You may already know which of the keys has the greatest impact on your mood, and be taking steps to make some changes. You may be aware that making physical changes – adjusting your diet, for example, or cutting out alcohol – makes the most difference to how you feel. If you are a people person, you may find that the relationships key is where your problems lie, and where the solutions can be found. But why not consider all of the options, and make changes in each of the key areas?

Today, we'll start by learning how to manage anxiety, and we'll look at a few strategies that will directly affect the way you feel. Some of the measures will also help you deal with depression, which we'll be looking at in more detail on day 12. The Mood-Maps below illustrate what we'll aim to achieve.

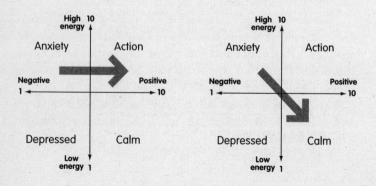

Changing Anxious to Action and Calm

We'll now work through the five keys to mood to establish some of the best ways to shift your anxiety to something more positive.

Key 1: Your surroundings

1. **Move!** Just moving from the place where you feel anxious to somewhere else can help you to feel calmer. In fact, even changing your chair can help. Your mind quickly starts to associate anxiety with a particular place and if you move, it helps to reduce your anxiety.

2. **Get outside.** Just going outside the front door to see the sky can help. If you have a quiet place near you, such as a church, museum, art gallery or library, go there and find a place to sit for a few minutes and reflect. And if the sun is shining, visit a park – sitting in the sunshine helps you to feel better. Even though you may want to stay inside where you feel safe and it is dark, you have to move if you want to change your mood.

3. **Spend time with nature.** Find a park or local beauty spot to walk in, near to trees, wildlife and water. The Bethlem Royal Hospital is set in acres of beautiful parkland and woods, with foxes, badgers, heron, even a flock of green parrots. While I was there, however bad I felt, walking in the grounds always made me feel better.

4. **Tidy up.** While your surroundings are a mess, you will be reminded of everything that you should but don't feel like doing. It is difficult to relax when you are surrounded by distractions. Anxiety affects memory. A floor-based system of filing may be good enough when you can remember where you put everything, but if your memory starts to fail, it becomes impossible. It is all too easy to spend large parts of each day looking for things. This makes anxiety worse. Start by sorting everything into big piles. Seeing the carpet again or the surface of your desk, helps you feel more in control.

5. **Create order.** Longer-term mood management requires order. A business depends on good people, using good systems. The same is true of a home. If you run things efficiently, your anxiety will begin to disperse.

6. **Get rid of unwanted and unused items.** The sight of half-started projects and ideas holds you back and prevents your life from moving forward. You will always be stuck in a place that is cluttered and reminds you of everything you want to shift. As the designer and poet William Morris once said, 'Have nothing in your house that you do not know to be useful or believe to be beautiful.'

7. **Create a quiet place.** Nothing encourages anxiety like anxiety! If there is nowhere you can go for some peace and quiet, you will never get a chance to settle down and calm your mood. Nowadays, houses tend to be open-plan 'machines for living', rather than being a refuge from the world. Find somewhere in your house that you can make into a quiet place – even if it is only part of a room – where you relax and keep one or two beautiful ornaments, photographs or plants.

8. **Change the scene.** If you are unhappy living somewhere, it may be time to move or at least redecorate. If your work distresses you, it may be time to look for a new job. Painful memories from the past can easily take control of your present mood.

9. **Make music.** More than any other external influence, music has a profound effect on how we feel. Music changes mood dramatically and in an instant. And think outside the box a little here. For example, if you don't normally like military music or marching bands, maybe it's time to reconsider as this type of music is excellent for addressing anxiety. It was developed to get men marching into battle at a time when battle wounds were likely to be fatal, pay was poor and life was grim. It worked then and still works now. The regular rhythm and upbeat tunes positively affect your mood even if you don't actually 'enjoy' listening to it.

WHICH STRATEGY WORKS FOR YOU?

You almost certainly already have a number of strategies that you use to take yourself from anxiety to action or from anxiety to calm. Make a list of what you already do to calm yourself down or get yourself going when you are feeling anxious. Beside each, note down when and how it has worked in the past, and how effective it is.

WHAT I DO WHEN I AM ANXIOUS	WHEN, HOW AND HOW EFFECTIVE
GO FOR A WALK	Useful, especially if I do not have anyone to talk to; have to concentrate on keeping my mind off my problems
TALK TO MY PARTNER	Useful, but not always fair to bother him with my problems; works best when I am feeling out of control
MUSIC	Always helps, but I often forget about it; works in most situations

There are many more examples of strategies to follow. When you come across a strategy that you find helpful, add it to your list in your notebook. This helps you build a resource that you can look at when you need to. In a crisis, it can often be difficult to remember what you know, but if you have the list to hand, you can remind yourself of what has worked in the past.

RALPH

Ralph had been burgled twice in his flat, and no longer felt comfortable there. He didn't want to move because the flat was convenient for his work and close to the shops. In order to manage his anxiety, he put new bolts and new locks on the windows and doors, and fitted a burglar alarm. But it was not until his girlfriend suggested redecorating that he was able to feel comfortable again, as he literally painted over his old associations. The new look in his apartment, combined with his increased security measures, enabled him to feel safe again.

Key 2: Your physical health

Anxiety produces as many physical as mental symptoms, and it is a physical state as much as it is a mood. By improving your physical health, you can increase your resilience or ability to cope, which will improve your mood, even when your underlying problems are unchanged.

ANXIETY IS MADE WORSE BY...

- Too much caffeine – in tea, coffee and cola. One or two cups of tea or coffee a day are more than enough for the average person. Some people are so sensitive that they need to avoid caffeine altogether.

- Fizzy drinks, which contain chemicals, additives, sweeteners and often caffeine, make anxiety worse and are best avoided completely.

- Sugar makes anxiety and moods swings worse. It is quickly absorbed from the gut and goes straight into the bloodstream. This raises the body's blood sugar levels, the body then produces insulin, and the blood sugar drops. As your blood sugar drops, you will feel tired, irritable and low. And as you repeat the sugar cycle, your mood becomes increasingly unstable.

- Alcohol plays havoc with blood sugar levels and makes us feel jumpy and anxious the next day.

- Pain makes anxiety worse – just as anxiety makes pain worse.

- Poor sleep, which is another double-edged sword. Anxiety makes sound sleep difficult, and lack of good-quality sleep can make you feel anxious.

- Lack of exercise. In a more natural world, anxiety would be a cue for physical action, whether it was sorting out a quarrel with a quick fight, or running away if you were frightened. Nowadays we suppress our physical reactions. This can lead to stress, anxiety and irritation, and lead us to feel aggressive, insecure and over-sensitive.

By now you will be familiar with the physical symptoms of anxiety, such as sweaty palms, muscle tension, headaches, cramping abdominal pain, fatigue, poor appetite and irritability, to name just a very few. You'll also know that anxiety makes many physical health problems worse, including eczema, IBS (irritable bowel syndrome), and even high blood pressure.

Here's how to make physical changes to shift your anxiety to something more positive.

1. **Breathing.** Anxiety brings on a pattern of rapid, short, shallow breathing. Controlling your breathing is the quickest way to control the physical symptoms of anxiety. Consciously slow your breathing, making sure that your breath comes from your belly. As you focus on calming your breathing, your anxiety will quickly reduce and you will start to think clearly again. This is especially important if you feel a panic attack coming on. Managing your breathing helps get rid of the 'paralysis' that often comes with extreme anxiety.

2. **Consciously relax.** If you act calm, and move calmly, you will find yourself calming down. In other words, 'fake it till you make it!' Let your shoulders relax. Shoulders should hang downwards and backwards, rather than being rounded or hunched – two postures seen commonly in stressed people. Walk in a relaxed manner, allowing your arms to hang loosely by your sides, swinging gently. Hold your head up, as though you have a balloon tied to the top of it.

3. **Exercise.** Movement helps to balance the body and it is the best antidote to the physical components of anxiety. The body needs to use up the energy of anxiety, and exercise is the healthiest way to do this. So get moving – go for a walk on your own or with friends, take a regular exercise class, swim, chase your dog, dance, join some friends for a game of golf, and use the stairs rather than the lift. As your anxious energy

is regularly dispersed, you'll experience a massive reduction in symptoms.

4. **Eat well.** The best advice is to eat for health, and you'll find details of how to do this on Day 7. If your blood sugar is kept steady, and your body is given the fuel it needs to operate efficiently, you'll experience enhanced well-being on all levels. Anxiety is exacerbated by poor physical health, and by erratic blood sugar levels.

5. **Use water.** This has almost magical properties to help reduce anxiety. Drink it, splash it on your face, bathe or shower in it, or even run through the sprinkler in the garden.

6. **Massage.** There can be no doubt that this feels *good*! Massage helps to remove tension from tired, stressed, tight muscles. In particular, massaging around your eyes and the sides of your neck can work wonders for anxiety.

Key 3: Your relationships

The people around us help to protect us from the worst excesses associated with our moods and our thinking. Humans are a social species, and throughout our lives we depend upon one another. The people around you can both cause and cure your anxiety. The following strategies will help get your mood moving towards Action and Calm.

1. **Talk about your problems.** When you talk to people about problems, you learn you are not alone, but if you sit on your own, it is easy get your difficulties out of proportion. Just finding the words to describe your experience makes it feel more normal and less extreme. With time, it becomes easier to handle.

2. **Get a good social network.** This helps us to balance our lives, and reduces anxiety. Research has found that being part of a group protects mental health. In contrast, people without

regular human contact become isolated, eccentric and unwell. Treasure your friends!

3. **Consider a self-help group.** The Doctors' Support Network is a self-help group for doctors with mental health problems. It has two mottos: 'To know you are not alone' and 'To learn to be kinder to oneself and others'. The strength of the network is based on meeting other doctors who have also had depression and mental health problems. This allows people to give mutual support and see that problems can be overcome. It also helps the members do something positive for themselves.

JASON

As a teenager, Jason had been depressed. He recovered, passed his 'A' levels and went on to complete a university degree in economics. When he started applying for jobs, he found that a common feature of many applications was the question: 'Do you have or have you ever had depression or another major mental health problem?' Jason worried that he might never get a job if his employers found out that he had suffered from depression. In his mind, the problem became overwhelming.

Finally Jason talked to a friend who was a couple of years older. It turned out that his friend had also been depressed as a teenager, and they could share their experiences. He reassured Jason that employers were more interested in a person's abilities than whether they had experienced depression as a teenager. After talking this over together, Jason realised that instead of worrying about the past, he needed to show his future boss how well he could do the job.

Key 4: Your knowledge

Your knowledge, or 'how you think' can either make your anxiety worse or help to solve the problem. In small doses, stress adds an edge to our performance – often increasing energy and enhancing creativity as you find new ways to achieve the impossible. But when stress is relentless, your energy and reserves start to become exhausted and problems start to seem insoluble. Anxiety and worry set in. The same thoughts keep going round in your mind, conversations keep going over the same ground and nothing changes. Your brain needs a bit of peace and quiet to sort out its problems.

By focusing on something different, you give your brain a chance to rest and work out its own solution, without continually being bothered by the conscious mind. Managing anxiety helps you manage your mood. Once your mood is better, your thinking improves.

The following strategies can help you to shift your anxiety, by working directly with your thoughts.

1. **Just stop!** The sooner you stop worrying, the easier it is. Worrying doesn't help! As with all habits, the longer you let it go on, the harder it is to change. A simple way to stop yourself worrying is to say the word 'STOP' out loud! (If there are people around, you may wish to say this loudly to yourself!) Saying 'STOP' silences your internal voice. This moment of silence gives you a chance to focus on something else.

2. **Thought-tagging.** Worry often takes the form of unhelpful questions, to which your brain provides equally unhelpful answers. If there is a crisis, your brain plays on your uncertainties and asks questions that cannot be answered. For example, if a friend is ill, or a boyfriend is unfaithful, the voice inside your head may ask 'What will happen to Jean?' or 'What is Brian doing tonight? He said he would phone.' No one knows the answers, and your imagination is given free rein to explore all the possibilities. Thought-tagging is a way to deal with these unanswerable questions. Find a tag that answers the question in a simple, straightforward way. For example, 'The doctors are doing their best to help Jean'

or 'Brian has reasons for his behaviour'. Every time the voice inside your head asks a question about Jean or Brian, you immediately give your answer. You 'tag' the thought. If you consistently 'tag' your thoughts, the voice inside your head gets bored and stops asking questions you cannot answer. Thought-tagging also means that you have a ready answer for the voice in your head, and you don't have to enter into discussion with this voice. See below for tips on putting this into practice.

3. **The worry hour.** There are occasions when the impulse to worry seems too powerful to resist, and despite the best thought-tagging, the 'voice inside your head' keeps throwing up new worries. On these occasions, it can help to put aside a set time each day – or even twice a day – to worry. If you have some major worries, set up a worry hour and make sure you keep your worries for your worry hour. If a worry comes to mind outside your worry hour, write it down and worry about it at the appointed time. The worry hour helps to stop your negative thoughts from getting out of hand.

4. **Keep track of time**. If you are having a worrying time and find you keep drifting off into anxiety, set an alarm to go off every half hour or so to remind you where you are. Use the alarm to 'wake you up', and if you are worrying, use a quick strategy to get back on track. For example, you might move from where you are sitting, get a glass of water, or listen to some music to change your mood. If you lose track of time, you can easily spend the whole day worrying.

5. **Inner critic to inner coach**. The voice inside your head gives you a running commentary of questions and comments and can, unless trained, be your worst critic. In many cases, the 'voice inside your head' has been programmed from your earliest years to be negative, and has picked up criticisms from parents, teachers, friends and everyone else. It then reminds you constantly of where you don't quite meet the grade.

You can, however, choose how you talk to yourself, and this involves choosing the right questions in order to get the right answers. For example, if you ask yourself 'How stupid can I be?' your voice will corroborate and say 'As stupid as usual... I wonder what stupid thing you'll come up with next?' However, if you ask yourself, 'What have I learnt?', 'How could I do this differently in the future?', or even 'What good could come of this?' you can start a useful conversation with yourself, and reframe things. The voice inside your head is one way that your brain communicates with you, and it is important to turn your inner critic into an inner coach, to support yourself, develop new ideas and deal with the people around you. A good coach doesn't tell you everything you

THOUGHT-TAGGING IN ACTION

Someone made a complaint about me at work. I became anxious, not least because I could not find out what the complaint was about, or who had made it. I started worrying. I then made up a thought tag, which went something like: 'Whatever happens to this complaint, I will learn from it.' Every time the voice inside my head mentioned the complaint, I repeated again, 'Whatever happens, I will learn from it.' After a while, the voice stopped bringing up the subject, as though it had got bored because I didn't react. And when I finally found out more about the complaint, I *did* learn from it. After a few days, I felt confident that I could deal with any consequences of the complaint. So much so, that when the complaint failed to materialise, I almost felt disappointed!

Different worries require different thought tags. For example, if you are worried about money, every time you think about it, you might add the thought tag: 'Learning to deal with this will help me to become rich.' Within a few days, your brain will get bored with those worries and may find different questions. The voice inside your head wants to talk – you can't stop it talking, but you can guide the conversation!

do is wrong; rather, he or she concentrates on what you do right and nudges you to improve. A good coach asks questions that help you to improve your insight and understanding.

Key 5: Your nature

Knowing who you are, and being able to express yourself, are vital for balanced mental health and feeling good. That's not to say that you can do what you want, whenever you want, without restrictions. But living constantly without being able to express yourself is stressful, and it's time that you did something about it. Here are some of the best ways to shift Anxiety to Calm or Action:

1. **Hold on to your vision.** If you know what you want to do, and you know where your talents lie, it's important to keep your vision in mind. This will help you to overcome all sorts of obstacles. Let's say, for example, that you want to be a journalist in the fashion industry, and get a job working at reception in a famous fashion magazine. Your boss is a bully and makes your life a nightmare. By remembering your vision, your boss's bullying becomes less important and less hurtful. You can hold your vision in mind and see his behaviour as a hurdle to cross, rather than an indictment against your character. You may feel a little stressed, but you won't be destroyed by this boss because you have a firm grip on what this job will give you in the future. You aren't going to let a boss stand in the way!

2. **Live according to your values.** Being true to yourself and your values enables you to be strong, regardless of what is going on around you.

3. **Be passionate!** Passion is the greatest antidote to anxiety. Being passionate about what you do, where you are, and who you are with is perhaps the single greatest key to a happy life. If you are doing something you are passionate about, there is very little that can stop you from achieving whatever you want.

WHICH MEDITATION?

- Transcendental meditation involves repeating a personal mantra. Mine, for example, was 'Kurin'. This is a meaningless word, and it was chosen for me by the man leading the class, but meaningless is good! It stops your brain from trying to impose meaning on a word when there is none, and this helps to clear your mind. As you repeat the mantra, you are able to observe what you are thinking, without engaging your thoughts. Instead, the thoughts are seen for what they really are – fleeting impulses that pass quickly. When viewed this way, thoughts are much more easily released.

- Mindful Meditation teaches you to direct your attention where you choose, rather than being constantly distracted by whatever catches your eye. You are taught to become more aware of what is happening in the moment – for example, what you can hear, what sensations you feel from your body, how warm or cold you are.

- Hypnosis, whether as hypnotherapy, hypnosis or autohypnosis, involves reaching a 'wakeful' state of focused attention, which is enormously relaxing. This is not, in the strictest sense, meditation; however, it does have a similar effect on your mind. It also has the effect of lowering energy and encouraging calm. It is more of a conscious process than meditation, and when you are feeling relaxed, you can use suggestions that are made to you to change the way you feel.

Obviously if you are anxious, it can be difficult to settle down to meditate; however, even a couple of minutes a day at the outset can make a difference to the way you feel, and start to encourage calm. Gradually, you can build up to longer periods of meditation each day, which will help to make calm a regular feature in your life.

4. **Have faith.** Faith – whether it represents a belief in God, or a greater cause or grander plan – is an antidote to anxiety. There is some evidence to suggest that faith in a better life gives you hope, certainty, confidence and a calm that can make the difference between carrying on and giving up when the going gets tough. It can make the difference between success and failure.

5. **Meditation.** This is a technique that helps people become calm. It is a way of focusing the mind – on breathing, on a beautiful object, on a word, or on what is happening in the moment. It is also a way of stopping the mind from chasing anxious thoughts and focusing on being calm. Like physical exercise, it needs to be done regularly for best results. There are many different types of meditation; some are more energetic than others, but all work to relax the mind and help you feel better (see page 154)

😦😊 **Day 11** Exercise

The strategies above will help you to shift away from anxiety towards a more positive calm or active mood. Remember that it can take time to use these strategies effectively; however, MoodMapping will help you to chart your progress.

We've learnt a great deal today, and there are many, many ways that you can reinforce the information you've learnt. The more you practise, the easier it will become to shift your mood, and the more you will realise that anxiety is a choice, and you can choose to change the way you feel. MoodMapping helps you see which strategies work best for you, and keep track of your progress.

As well as learning to manage your anxiety, it is equally important to tackle the problems that have caused it. You may be clear about the cause already, or it may be a general feeling that doesn't seem to be related to anything. Remember that all anxiety has a cause, and looking at the different areas of your life in detail can help to ascertain what's causing yours.

Next, you'll find a few different exercises to get you started on the road to reducing anxiety. Each builds on the strategies learnt in this chapter, and can be undertaken on its own or along with the others. Don't forget to chart your progress with your MoodMap.

Find your inner coach

The first stage in transforming your inner critic into a supportive coach is to create some ground rules. For example:

1. Never say anything to yourself that you would not say to a good friend.

2. Criticism is allowed, but it must be constructive.

3. Respect yourself.

4. If you are rude, apologise to yourself.

Criticism is fine, because none of us is perfect. We improve with constructive criticism. However, it *must* be helpful for it to be effective; anything hurtful will simply undermine the process. So, all criticism must be sandwiched between praise.

Every time you feel that you have done something wrong, or you become anxious, stop and coach yourself through the proceedings. Take a step back and be honest but fair. What was good? (You may have to work hard to find this, but it is there, I promise you!) What was not so good? What good things did you undertake to deal with it? Finally, ask yourself what you have learnt.

Always sandwich two good points on either side of a 'less good' point. For example, let's say you drop a cup and stain your new white rug. What was good? Well, you may have been tidying up, which is good. In other words, your motives were good. What's not so good? You dropped the cup! What did you do to deal about it? You cleared up quickly and managed to remove most of the stain. Finally, you've learnt to slow down a little, and take things more slowly.

Instead of allowing your inner critic to say, 'You idiot! What were you trying to do? You were running late and now look at what's happened!', you can use your inner coach to show yourself some calm respect, which can be built on. Treat yourself as you would a friend or a respected colleague. It really *matters* how you speak to yourself. Silence that critic, and apologise for being rude. Allow your inner coach to encourage you to come away from the experience feeling good about yourself, and positive about not repeating the same things in future.

How you speak to people and how you treat them is the difference between a good relationship and one that hurts both sides. Self-talk is about giving yourself the same respect you give your best friend, because whether you like you or not, you have to live with you for the rest of your life! The trick to getting on with people is to focus on their good points.

So start now. Have a 'conversation' with yourself at appointed times throughout the day, and keep it positive, complimentary and upbeat. Note down in your notebook how these exchanges made you feel. You'll soon see that great moods can stem from great self-talk.

Face your fears and make a plan

Uncertainty is a major cause of anxiety. Not knowing what will happen fuels your worries. As soon as you know what to expect, anxiety tends to disappear, leaving you feeling calm. You may not be happy with the result, but once that 'unknown' element is removed, you can get on and deal with it.

So removing the 'unknown' is important, and this means facing your fears – imagining and facing the worst possible outcome for any situation, and realising that you *can* cope.

Draw a table with three columns, and then list your problems or challenges in the left-hand column. Next, describe the worst possible outcome, and then work out how you would handle it.

Your table may look something like this:

PROBLEM OR CHALLENGE	WORST POSSIBLE RESULT	WHAT I WOULD DO IF THE WORST HAPPENED
Not finishing the manuscript for the book	Lose contract and have to find a new publisher	I would carry on and finish the manuscript and get the book published, even if I had to do it myself
Difficult relationship at work	Lose job because of the difficulties caused to employer	Find a new job working in a different department. Work hard to get a promotion so I don't find myself in the same position again
Having difficulty paying credit card bills	Go bankrupt and lose home	Find somewhere else to live, learn about money and make sure I am never in that position again

If you can face the worst that could happen to you and know you can cope, there is nothing to make you anxious.

Day 12:
Escaping depression

God grant me the serenity to accept the
things I cannot change;
courage to change the things I can;
and wisdom to know the difference.

'THE SERENITY PRAYER', REINHOLD NIEBUHR

Today, we'll look at the best ways to shift depression. This is a different challenge from letting go of anxiety, because depression tends to be characterised by a complete lack of energy. When you are anxious, you do have a certain energy, albeit unpleasant, which can be harnessed to make changes; however, when you are depressed it can seem impossible to do anything at all.

For this reason, I suggest that our first goal is to shift your mood from 'bottom left' (depressed), to 'bottom right' (calm). Once you have rested and recuperated in a calm state, you'll be better placed to motivate yourself to shift from calm to action. If you try to move directly from depressed to action, you can make impossible demands on your energy and well-being, leading to an unstable mood.

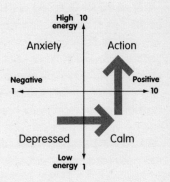

It's important to remember that there is a reason for exhaustion and depression, just as anxiety has a cause. When you are depressed, however, it can be very difficult to see for yourself what is obvious to the rest of the world. For example, I saw a mother of three children, who had a full-time job and a partner who worked away from home most of the week. She could not understand why she was feeling depressed. I'm pretty sure that almost everyone else could.

Remember, too, that the cause may not always be in the present. It may often be the case (particularly if you have had an emotionally difficult past) that your depression has as much to do with memories and association as it does with what's going on now. Depression is a deep tiredness, where the spring has gone from your soul. It has many causes, from hard work, repeated disappointment, living in an unsafe environment for too long, and lack of family or friendly support to poor physical health.

But humans heal! Your mind and body can recover, even if it takes a little time. So, if your mood is not improving with time, there has to be a reason. For example, if you have been bullied at work and this caused you to be depressed, once the situation has been sorted out, your mood should improve. If your mood does

MEDICATION

Doctors and, indeed, depressed patients, often assume that medication is the answer to depression, and that a course of treatment will open the shutters and let the light in for good. This may indeed be the case for severe depression; however, it is open to debate how valuable medication is for mild and moderate depression. While some people undoubtedly find it helpful, despite the side-effects, it can be more productive to work on making changes instead – which will not only be longer-lasting, but will also provide you with a series of strategies for changing your depressive mood. Most of us like to feel that we are, to some extent, in control, and having these tools at your disposal can be much more effective than simply taking medication that goes nowhere towards addressing the root cause.

not improve, there has to be a reason. It may be that you are experiencing bullying in other areas of your life. You may have poor health, which could also have been caused by the stress of the bullying. Perhaps you have a legacy of poor self-esteem from the past, so that you continue to beat yourself up with damaging self-talk, even though the external bully has been removed.

Changing Depressed to Calm and Action

Many of the strategies described for anxiety also work for depression, and will help you to change an anxious mood. Let's look at them in order of the five keys to mood.

Key 1: Your surroundings

Where you live and operate will affect your mood, and never more than in the case of depression. If you live in depressing surroundings, you will struggle to feel anything but depressed. The old Victorian asylums may, in retrospect, seem a little grim, and not exactly replete with creature comforts, but they were often set in beautiful grounds, which the Victorians rightly believed helped people to regain their mental health.

This came home to me when I was working in general practice in South London. Although many council estates are well run, some are not good places, especially if you have children. I remember one mother who had two lively young children and lived on one such estate. Every morning, almost regardless of the weather, she took her children to a nearby park for half an hour, so that the children could play outside and she could sit and enjoy the trees and the grass. She started doing it at the suggestion of her community health worker, after she had experienced a period of depression. Her children got some exercise and she was able to enjoy a little bit of nature. The Victorians gave many parks to our towns and we can still enjoy their benefits today. Even if we don't have children or a dog to walk, these are places that help us reconnect with our more natural instinctive selves.

1. **Soak up the sunlight.** Many people become depressed in winter (a condition known as Seasonal Affective Disorder, or SAD). This appears to be caused by a lack of sunlight, which has a profound impact on chemicals in the brain. Sunlight can, in fact, help with depression no matter what the season. It increases the level of melatonin in our brains and this seems to improve the natural rhythms of the brain, which makes us feel better. Take half an hour to walk outside at lunchtime, or sit in your garden or the local park for a little while each day. A light box or visor (see page 106) can be a useful alternative, if you just can't get outside. If you can afford it, a holiday in the sun during the winter months can make a huge difference to the way you feel, and prevent mild depression from becoming something more deep-seated.

2. **Lift your spirits with music.** Music in depression is interesting. Many people play sad songs in order to feel better, whether it is sad love songs, or something by Leonard Cohen. And in a strange way this works. I used to play 'Everybody Hurts' by REM all the time. By echoing how you feel, music seems to exorcise the ghosts. Once the music echoes your mood, you can gradually play more cheerful tracks. Use music to meet your despair, then gradually lead it somewhere more hopeful.

3. **Keep photos of the people you love.** Studies show that people who survived against the odds – who were, for example, stranded in the desert because their vehicle had broken down – survived by remembering people they loved. Keep photos of your family, your children or your favourite niece or nephew close to you. These are physical reminders of the good in life. When I was in a psychiatric hospital, the mother of a patient whom I had treated following a severe head injury sent photographs of her daughter's wedding. Seeing how beautiful her daughter was, and reading about how she had restarted her studies and was now qualified, reminded me that the brain heals, as long as we give it a chance. This helped my recovery because the picture reminded me that I too could get better.

4. Start a little garden. This is about creating life. Either use a corner of your own garden or, if you live in flat, use the balcony or even just an indoor pot to nurture some plants. Working with soil seems to connect us with our environment; and tending plants and watching them grow reminds us of the miracle of life.

Key 2: Your physical health

Good physical health encourages your mind and your brain to recover from depression. Exercise and a healthy diet both have well-proven mental health benefits.

1. **Avoid toxins, stimulants and depressants.** In a nutshell, this means sugar, caffeine, nicotine, alcohol and food additives. It might seem impossible to rid your diet of all these things, but the more you cut down, the better you feel. There is some evidence that people prone to depression are more sensitive to chemicals, so give the harmful ones a miss.

2. **Up your oils.** A large number of studies show the benefits of omega 3 fish oils, in particular on mental function and well-being. Professor Basant Puri, Dr Andrew Stoll and Dr Michael Peet have undertaken studies on the benefits of omega 3 fish oils for depression and other mental-health problems.

3. **Stabilise your blood sugar.** You can do this by cutting out sugar-laden and processed foods, and making sure most of your diet is based around whole, unrefined foods. When your blood sugar levels soar and plunge, your mood follows suit.

4. **Go for simple.** Simple, unprocessed foods will give you more energy and balance your moods. What's more, simple, easy-to-digest foods are ideal when you are suffering from depression – largely because you don't have the energy or inclination to prepare anything more complicated, nor, perhaps, the appetite to eat it. Try smoothies, mint tea, bananas, warming vegetable broths and soups, all of which will give you a nutrient boost, but avoid putting pressure on your system.

5. **Memory food.** Foods are often associated with comfort and good times. Which foods bring back good memories? Is there a dish that your mum used to make, which still makes you feel safe and secure? Macaroni cheese, perhaps, or cottage pie. Add it to your diet! Or what about a paella, just like the one you had on your uplifting holiday in Spain?

6. **Eat raw.** Have plenty of fruit, nuts and sprouting seeds, raw vegetables such as tomatoes and carrots, honey, lemon, ginger and dark chocolate. These foods contain naturally occurring chemicals that help improve your overall health – and improve your mood!

7. **A little exercise.** Physical exercise is difficult when you are depressed, and depression or a low mood does affect physical performance. I used to monitor my mood depending on how far I could swim. Yet, even if you can only manage a short walk at lunchtime, it is worth the effort in terms of improving your mood. Once again, exercise gets those endorphins going – the natural feel-good chemicals in your brain (see pages 37, 100-1).

8. **Finger-dancing.** Any kind of movement helps to lift depression, even if it is not formal exercise. Try finger-dancing! Tap and move your fingers around in time to your favourite piece of music. It's a little bit of easy fun, and the music and movement gently stimulate your brain.

9. **Smile!** Smiles are good for your mood. Smile at yourself in the mirror – you'll experience the benefits of both smiling *and* having someone smile back at you!

Key 3: Your relationships

More perhaps than any other key to mood, supportive relation-ships can help you through a period of depression. Friends and family matter most during hard times. On the other hand, if there are people in your life who are not supportive, or who damage your self-esteem, keep out of their way if you can.

1. **Clear out your contact book.** Although many of us cling on to friendships come hell or high water, it's important to remember that not all friendships are meant to be. If there are people in your life who undermine you, regularly upset you, and zap your energy, it's time to make some changes.

2. **Change the way you look at your family relationships.** Obviously you can't choose your family, but you can teach them to be more supportive. Alternatively, you might have to lower your expectations and accept that the familial relationship can be a tricky one – and that you are not alone on that front!

3. **Friends for each 'mood'.** I have friends whose company I enjoy when I am feeling strong, but who are not helpful to have around when I am feeling down. Learn to spend time with people who boost you when you are feeling low; similarly, avoid friends who compound the feeling. Even if it's just a short-term measure, it can help you to keep control of your moods.

4. **Getting out.** It can be tempting to lock yourself away when you are too low and tired to engage with people; however, isolation can make depression worse, whereas a sense of belonging can make a difference to your mood. Just being with people helps. It is, for example, better to go out to the cinema and sit with warm bodies around you than it is to sit at home on your own watching television.

5. **Talk, talk, talk.** It helps to talk to people. Whether you phone a friend, a member of your family, or a helpline, it can be uplifting simply to hear a friendly voice on the other end of the line. Good friends can make you feel better, regardless of what is going on around you.

Key 4: Your knowledge

The way you think when you are down can become a self-fulfilling prophecy. If you think you are doing badly, it is all too easy for those thoughts to become real. What's more, they can begin a cycle of negative thoughts and negative events from which it can be hard to escape. However, the opposite is also true. If you think positively, and continually nurture positive thoughts, you can change both your mood and the way you see yourself and your life.

1. **Positive self-talk.** How you talk to yourself matters. When you are feeling down is not the time to remind yourself of your faults. Go easy on yourself, and never say anything to yourself that you would not say to the person closest to you. So, instead of saying 'I am a bad person', try 'I may not do everything right, but I do what I can, as well as I can'. Or instead of saying 'I am so stupid!', try 'I might not have been bright at school, but I have common sense and I can think my way out of most situations'. It is easy to think that we do not deserve the common courtesy that we give to other people. I used to ask the fire-fighters how they thought someone would feel if they were subject to the same barrage of criticism they heap on themselves. 'Terrible' was the answer. I then asked them if they could see a connection between how they felt and how they talked to themselves. It was a lightbulb moment!

2. **Cognitive Behaviour Therapy (CBT).** Depressive thinking is a frame of mind where you see yourself as a failure, the world as unfriendly, and the future as grim. Cognitive Behaviour Therapy offers the best opportunity to change this thinking. It encourages people to challenge their negative thinking, and break unhealthy patterns. It can be hard work when you are feeling depressed, but if you go gently it can start to change your thinking.

3. **Incantations.** In a low mood, you may not have a lot of energy for self talk but it can help to have a set of stock phrases that you can bring out when you need to. An incantation is a phrase that you repeat to yourself regularly. It requires no effort to bring it to mind and it contains a phrase that means something to you. For example, you could 'incant': 'This too

will pass', 'Each day is better', or 'I will come through'. One that had particular personal meaning for me while I was in hospital was 'Remember the Light'. This saying reminded me of the beautiful dawn I had seen on the morning I was admitted to hospital. It was almost two months after that before I was allowed outside to see and feel the sunshine again.

Use incantations regularly throughout the day to remind yourself that your depression is temporary – that it is not the real you, and that the way you feel is just a reflection of your present mood. You might find it useful to note down a list of phrases you find helpful. Each day choose one or two phrases to repeat to yourself throughout the day. If nothing else, it helps to put a positive spin on things, and helps to change a gloomy outlook.

4. **Pay someone a compliment.** It can often be difficult to find things to talk about when you are feeling depressed. If you want to make conversation but you can't think of anything to say, just say something nice. Everyone likes a compliment, and the positive energy you create will help you to feel better!

5. **Read inspirational quotes.** When you are feeling depressed, it is difficult to finish even a short magazine article. Instead, look for short quotes that can help you feel better. Many internet sites offer a daily service of inspirational quotes. A short saying is easier to read than an article, and can lift your mood immeasurably.

Key 5: Your nature

Depression comes out of adversity. People who have never experienced difficulties or struggled for anything worthwhile do not become depressed. Depression does not come out of the blue, and there are reasons for the way you are feeling – even if those reasons are sometimes difficult to identify. Four key words can help lift depression and immediately improve your mood. These are acceptance, forgiveness, gratitude and hope. As you practise employing these words, use your MoodMaps to continue checking that what you are doing is working.

1. **Accept.** Whatever has happened in the past is over. It has happened, no matter how difficult that may be to come to terms with. But acceptance is key to lifting mood. Being able to make sense of what happened, learn from it, and then put it firmly in the past will allow you to move forward. It can be very hard to accept your reality, particularly if it isn't what you'd like it to be. Many of us race round in circles denying that things have happened, never shouldering any blame, and keeping hurt and bad memories alive. If you stop, accept and then move on, you release a whole pot of energy that would otherwise be used in the pursuit of the impossible. You can't change the past, but you can change the future. It took me almost 10 years to accept that I had a diagnosis of bipolar disorder. Accepting my diagnosis caused depression, because it meant that I could not carry on as I had in the past – pretending nothing was wrong. However, until I accepted the diagnosis, I could not work on a solution. Nothing can turn the clock back; the best we can do is to make the most of what we have at this moment, now. That means accepting who we are, where we are, and then moving on.

2. **Forgive.** A study from South Africa looked at how well three groups of people coped after being tortured under apartheid. The first group made a public appearance in front of the Truth and Reconciliation Commission. The second group presented their cases privately to the commission, while the third group was made up of people who chose not to appear before the commission. The study found that the most important difference between the people who had come to terms with what had happened and those who were still in difficulties, was whether or not they were able to forgive the person who had tortured them. Frankly, if people who have been tortured

under apartheid can forgive their torturers, we should most definitely be able to forgive those who have hurt us. There is no reason to keep replaying bad experiences in our minds, churning up feelings of hate and reinforcing our feelings of hurt. This study found that forgiveness helps people to gain wisdom and strength, and to move forward. Like many people, I spent many years being angry with my parents, on whom I blamed, amongst other things, my bipolar illness. When I finally forgave them for all of their real and imagined crimes, my mental health improved significantly. Holding on to resentment and bitterness does not help you.

3. **Be grateful.** I have a friend who says, 'Every day above ground is a good day.' It's a lovely optimistic thought, but, realistically speaking, life *can* be tough. It *can* be hard to find the little moments that make life worth living. Gratitude takes practice and persistence. It's easy to think that you have absolutely nothing to be grateful for, and that your life is awful; however, that depressive thinking is more a reflection of your state of mind than a reflection of the reality. Start small. Be grateful you didn't get a parking ticket when you were late back to your car, grateful that your friends remembered your birthday, grateful that the sun is shining. Being grateful for the little things can make the difference on the ground!

4. **Hope!** In depression and, indeed, any difficult circumstances, finding hope is the key. Some days I struggle with hope – particularly when I look around and see other people's greed, or pollution, or other big issues. Equally, however, I look around and see people who have a vision for their lives and for the world that fills me with hope. Beyond anything we do for ourselves, our legacy depends on the contribution we make to the lives of other people. So collective hope is important. Important, too, is your individual hope. Never ever give up hope. It's what keeps the fires of your soul burning. There is *every* chance that things will work out better in the future, and if you hang on to that, you'll keep those flames alive.

😣😊 Day 12 Exercise

Some of us have to work on gratitude, particularly in the deepest depression. However, it can help to undertake the following exercise, which will create a healthy habit of being grateful. This will undoubtedly change your mood, and the way you see the world around you.

Each day for a week, write down three things you have to be grateful for. With practice, you will find you can fill a page a day. Better still, even if the material facts of your life do not change, you will start to feel differently about life in general.

For example, today I am grateful...

- For the hour of sunshine at lunchtime

- That my phone did not ring so I could finish my report

- That my nephew passed his degree

- For that warm shower this morning

- For my cats

Being grateful is the habit of appreciation – of the big and little things in your life and in the world around you. It is important that you are convinced of this! By regularly mapping your mood before and after each exercise, you can see if it has helped to lift your mood even one point on the scale.

Day 13:
Escaping the anxiety/ depression loop

In life you need either inspiration or desperation.

ANTHONY ROBBINS

All too often, people become stuck in a cycle of anxiety and depression.

Unresolved anxiety – particularly occurring over long periods of time – is exhausting. With that exhaustion comes depression. Depression forces us to slow down and even stop, which has the effect of encouraging a partial recovery. However, because nothing has really changed, that depression is immediately replaced by anxiety, and the whole cycle starts all over again. This cycle of stress and anxiety followed by burnout, exhaustion and depression is all too common. If you recognise this mood pattern in yourself, you will also recognise the need to change. There are, happily, quite a few things you can do to break the cycle. Let's look at them today.

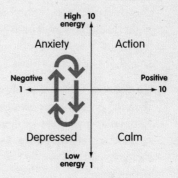

Strategies to escape the anxiety/depression loop

This is a destructive mood pattern and, more than any other mood state, you need to find the cause or causes of your present mental state. There are very likely challenges in at least two, or perhaps even all five of your mood keys. In the short term, you may not be able to address more than one or two areas; however, once you begin to unravel your mood, you will find that you can embrace many more changes while on the road to recovery. The exercise at the end of this chapter will help you to work out which challenges need to be sorted, and how you can go about doing so.

Key 1: Your surroundings

Whatever your mood, your surroundings are important.

1. **Make a hug spot to curl up in.** This is a place where you can snuggle up comfortably with a few favourite objects and sit quietly. Find a pillow you like, and place a sprig of aromatic, relaxing herbs inside. Dress in clothes that make you feel comfortable, and then head to your hug spot. This is not a place where you go to feel miserable, but somewhere you go to give yourself a hug! And when you feel better, you can get up and face the world again.

2. **Spend time listening.** Turn off the radio, your telephone and the TV, and spend time listening to the silence. In the early evening and early morning, listening for birdsong. The dawn chorus can lift your spirits, and perhaps make up for a restless night. Even the sound of distant traffic can help you to feel less alone. The world is bursting with soothing and uplifting sound, if you stop to listen.

3. **Go classical.** Classical music seems to come from a calmer time than the music of our own generation. If you normally listen to popular music, classical music can give you a different way of experiencing the world. Life may not have been easy but, in the past, perhaps people had more reasonable expectations of themselves.

PROFESSIONAL THERAPY

The anxiety/depression cycle can be enormously destructive, and you may find that professional therapy can make all the difference at the outset. Cognitive behavioural therapy can be helpful to break patterns and re-establish healthy habits and ways of thinking. You may, however, wish to find a therapy that looks more deeply into what has led you to this point. In particularly, a more psychoanalytically based therapy should prove invaluable.

The cycle of anxiety and depression will have taken time to develop. In many cases, people experiencing continually negative moods have deeper-seated problems that prevent them from feeling good, no matter what they try. In this case, it is useful to spend time with a professional, to find out what has caused you to feel this way.

I once had a young patient who had just finished university. She had a good degree and went straight into a new job. However, she found it increasingly difficult to cope. After talking to her, it was apparent that she had experienced a number of problems from a young age. Her parents were putting a lot of pressure on her to marry her boyfriend and settle down to have children. Because she was still young, she was torn between a sense of obligation to her parents, and her own desires and needs. As a result, she became anxious, with episodes of depression. She didn't think she would *ever* feel better, despite doing all that she could to keep her mood up. It was not until she started regular therapy with an experienced therapist that she could see her position clearly. Her therapist gave her a chance to talk about difficult subjects in a safe environment, and this allowed her to negotiate a course between her parents' expectations and her own needs.

It's important to acknowledge when you need a little help. If no strategies appear to be having anything more than a transient effect, it may be time to get some professional assistance. Deep-seated, long-term problems can take much longer to unravel, and there's nothing like having support while you go through the process.

4. **Watch the sky.** Look at the clouds – their different shapes and textures. See how fast they are moving, their colour variations and how high or low they are flying. Watch the birds, too. The light and movement will help you to feel better, and remind you that whatever happens in your own daily life, the planet will continue to move and change.

Key 2: Your physical health

Go oily. Fish, that is! Oily fish, such as herring, mackerel and salmon have been proven to boost mood and encourage emotional well-being. And their oils, rich in omega 3s, will also do the trick. If you aren't already doing so, make sure you get a good omega 3 supplement every day.

1. **Take a step back.** While it's tempting to do everything you can while you have some energy, you will only exhaust yourself. Make sure you relax regularly, and leave something in reserve in order to build yourself back up again. Do just enough to get you through the day.

2. **Have a massage.** Although it can be expensive, a deep massage is the best way to get tension out of your muscles, and it acts as an instant pick-me-up. When you feel better physically, your mind is in a better place to sort out your problems. There is plenty of evidence, too, that the power of touch is restorative.

3. **Walk in the night-time air.** Two hours before you go to bed, before it gets dark, go for a walk in the fresh air. This will help you to sleep better. Restorative sleep will allow you to waken refreshed, and in a better state of mind to sort out your problems. While you are walking, keep your ears pricked for the sounds going on around you. Can you hear distant birdsong? Trains or cars? The murmur of conversation? Focusing on something else will help to take your mind off your own state of affairs.

4. **Find your herbal essence.** Place a pillow stuffed with dried herbs near to your bed. Lavender, marjoram and rose are good choices, as they will encourage relaxation and restful sleep.

Key 3: Your relationships

While your mood fluctuates between anxiety and depression, it is difficult to know what you want from people, and it is equally tempting not to talk to anyone at all. This is the worst thing you can do. Don't be afraid to ask people to help you. It can often seem easier to get on with doing something on your own, but most people, given a chance, want to help their friends.

1. **Tell people how you feel.** The difficulty with a changing mood is that people do not know what to expect, so part of the strategy is to tell people how you feel. If they know what's coming, they'll be more likely to understand your mood patterns and shifts. What's more, they may be able to share details of similar experiences. Very few people lead even, trouble-free lives.

2. **Choose the right friend.** Do you need cheering up or do you need to deal with your anxiety? Who understands your situation? All of us have friends who are great in a crisis, and others who are positively uplifting. Choose the friend you need most when you need it most. Furthermore, even when it feels as though you are overwhelmed by your moods, keeping up to date with what is happening with your friends can help you to focus on the outside world. Spend time listening, and their moods will rub off on you.

3. **Use social networks to make contact with people.** Twitter, Facebook, texting and email are easy ways to keep in contact with your friends. Just put a message up so people know how you feel and what to expect. More than anything else, those around you can help you get your mood straightened out.

4. **Get physical.** It's important to see friends in person, and to spend physical time with the people you care about. Nothing replaces the physical boost of a quick hug or even just a pat on the shoulder. What's more, mood spreads more quickly when you are physically together. Take advantage of your friends' good moods to lift your own.

5. **Laugh with people.** Finding something to laugh about is what friends are for! Even in the grimmest circumstances, it is possible to find something that can make you smile. The idea that 'laughter is the best medicine' hasn't changed since the days of Hippocrates, so follow his advice.

Key 4: Your knowledge

When your mood swings between anxiety and depression, poor management of your energy is often at the root. It's a hard lesson to learn, but you simply have to become accustomed to conserving your energy whenever you have it, in order to prevent a return to depression. Below you'll find a list of strategies that are extremely effective. Some may work better than others for you, so continue to use your MoodMaps to ascertain how well they are working. Depression and anxiety put you in a strange frame of mind, and what might work ordinarily may leave you cold during difficult periods. If you have a list of things that work 'no matter what', you'll find it easier to shift your mood and conserve the energy you need to get and stay well again.

1. **Assess your expectations.** It's important that you continually assess your expectations of both yourself and those around you. If your standards and expectations are too high, everything and everyone will always fall short – including you! This is a recipe for disaster. Be realistic about your expectations. For example, if you are a person who demands a spotless home, consider the fact that it may be impossible to expect yourself to keep it that way with a brood of messy kids and a full-time job. Similarly, it is unrealistic to expect your

messy kids to be eternally tidy and clean! Your expectations need to change, even if it means adjusting your standards a little.

2. **Stop before you become tired.** This is an important habit to develop. When you are experiencing this state, you may be pleased simply to get anything at all done. When depression lifts enough to achieve something, you may also find that you push yourself too hard to make up for lost time. But this really is the most counter-productive thing you can do. Leave some little notes around the house to remind yourself of this fact. For example, leave a little note on your computer that says 'Just because I can doesn't mean I have to'. Alternatively, use a post-it to remind yourself to 'always leave some fuel in the tank to get home safely'. Getting out of the depression/anxiety loop means storing up some energy so you can start to move towards Action – a more positive mood. This is only possible when you have built up some reserves.

3. **Create a little quiet.** Have a quiet time each day, when you spend a moment just enjoying something you *enjoy*! You might focus on something in your house or, if you are at work, on your desk. Allow yourself to be distracted by thinking where it came from, what's in it, and how it got to be what it is. This gentle curiosity allows your brain to switch off from your everyday life, and catch up with itself.

4. **Expand your mind.** This sounds a little daunting, but it can be very therapeutic. The human mind is always asking new questions, and seeking new information. So spend a couple of minutes every day doing something that you don't need to do – finding out something for its own sake. This will take your mind away from your immediate situation, and also excite your curiosity, setting you off in new directions.

Key 5: Your nature

1. **Meditate.** Meditation is useful both in depression and in anxiety. It helps to bring about a calm state of mind, where you are able to look at your life more objectively, and get the strength you need to make changes. Start with a minute and a half. If you have not done anything like this before, find a clock with a second hand and do nothing more than sit quietly – watching the second hand move through your 90 seconds. Nothing short of a house fire should disturb these few seconds that are yours. As you watch the second hand, notice whether it moves smoothly or in a series of little jerks. Listen to it. Does it make a sound? Does it make the same sound every second, or is it slightly different? Does it make a sound as it moves or between the moves? As you get more used to sitting quietly, you can gradually increase the time you spend doing this. To begin with, it may seem like a waste of time. You have to take this one on trust, at least to start with, but over time, you will gain the mental discipline to be able to still your mind, and treasure the few minutes that are truly your own. And with this stilling comes creativity and a different approach.

2. **Be creative.** If you are having a difficult time, explore some creative options. A diary can be a great creative and therapeutic outlet. Just writing down what's happened to you each day can help you to feel better. If you are more visual and prefer pictures to words, you might try drawing or painting, even if you have never picked up a pen or a paintbrush before. Art is all about expressing your ideas through a picture, rather than using words, and it has a language of its own. There's no doubt that it works; art therapies can be enormously effective in reaching people who have lost the ability to express themselves.

3. **Stroke an animal.** Many studies confirm that having a pet helps you to live longer and protects your mental health. Many people describe how looking after an animal helps them focus on looking after themselves when they might otherwise not bother. If you have a pet, you cannot afford to be ill. Better still, animals know immediately how you feel and respond to your energy rather than your words. They also seem to know whether you are being honest about your feelings or whether you are trying to fool yourself into thinking you are fine when you are not. Studies have shown that people's blood pressure comes down and their pulse rate reduces when they stroke their pet. You may not feel able to look after a pet at present, but you can borrow friends' pets or offer to take their dog for a walk. Even watching tropical fish can be soothing.

Day 13 Exercise

When you are alternating between depression and anxiety, it is easy to feel overwhelmed by what is happening in your life. If you can prioritise your problems and find some small ways to make life better, you'll have the impetus you need to break the anxiety/depression loop.

Sitting down to list your challenges and difficulties may, in the short term, make you feel worse. However, sorting out even one or two difficulties may help you feel a great deal better and give you the energy and confidence you need to carry on the process. This exercise will not sort out your life completely, but it will provide a toehold with which to begin the process of change. Before you start, it may help to look back to your 'elephants' exercise (see page 127), to get a better idea of where you want to be.

Draw four columns in your notebook. Label the first 'major challenge', the second 'outcome', the third 'who to talk to', and the final column 'next step'.

Next, write down your three most significant challenges in the first column. It may take several attempts before you know exactly which three difficulties you want most to sort out. For example, you may want to move house, but may not be able to until you find a new job, or until your partner is also at a stage where he or she can also move. Brainstorm the list, perhaps with your partner or a friend, until you have discovered the three challenges you would most like to address.

Your list might look something like this:

MAJOR CHALLENGE	OUTCOME	WHO TO TALK TO	NEXT STEP
Credit card debts			
Relationship problems with new boyfriend			
Difficult position at work because of new manager			

Work out what you would like to happen in each area. This is your desired 'outcome'. What would you like to happen? How would you like the situation to be resolved? What is a reasonable expectation, given your circumstances, the time and the talents that you have?

Next, work out who you can talk to. Be specific here, and choose someone who will either have the resources to give you the support you need, or the knowledge or skills to help facilitate change. With their help, you can come up with the next step. You may even come up with some possible solutions yourself, so jot these down and use them as a starting point.

Your table may start to look something like this:

MAJOR CHALLENGE	OUTCOME	WHO TO TALK TO	NEXT STEP
Credit card debts	Be free of debt	Brother	Get card debt into a larger cheaper loan
Relationship problems with new boyfriend	Know if this relationship is right and get settled in a stable relationship	My aunt Jemma, who knows me, has good insight into people and relationships, and knows people who have seen us together	Talk to Jemma
Difficult position at work because of new manager	Be in a job that I can manage, which lets me work with people without too much management responsibility	Tony, a previous manager with whom I got on well	Talk to the new manager about what I do best and where I struggle

Concentrate on your three major challenges until you have at least one in manageable shape. Then work down the list until you've satisfactorily resolved them all. Three is plenty to begin with, and you can add to this list as you go on.

Use this table as a template for change, and continually update it as your plans progress. It's also a good idea to use MoodMapping to monitor your progress and to see when you switch from depression to anxiety and back.

Look back at the strategies that can help you manage Depression and Anxiety and see which ones might help you best to manage your mood.

Day 14:
Managing positive energy

Apathy can be overcome by enthusiasm, and enthusiasm can only be aroused by two things: first, an ideal, which takes the imagination by storm, and second, a definite intelligible plan for carrying that ideal into practice

ARNOLD TOYNBEE

This is a good problem! Life is good, but you still need to manage your energy. There is no point in owning the best racehorse in the world, unless you can train him to run his fastest. And the same applies to you. Today, we are going to look at how you can best channel your positive energy, so that your moods remain stable and you feel and operate at your best.

I have shown the mood map to a number of happy and successful people. Almost all of them estimated that they spend 90 per cent of their time on the positive side of the map. If you spend most of your time on the right side of the graph, you need to be able to manage your energy. Too much time in 'top right', and you risk making irrational decisions and indulging in impulsive behaviour. Too much time in 'bottom right', and nothing gets done.

The Tibetan people are a wonderful, generous and wise nation, where meditation is widely practised. They spend a lot of time in 'bottom right' but this has come at a cost because in 1950 the Chinese came and took their country.

Finding a balance

As with everything, the answer lies in the balance. You want to be able to balance activity with calm, and energy with rest and recovery. If you fail to rest when you are in 'action' for too long, it's all too easy to slip into anxiety and, from there, exhaustion and depression.

Equally, once you have learnt to achieve calm, it can be tempting to stay there! After all, what will any of this matter in a year's time, five years' time or fifty years' time? Surely it is better to enjoy the sunshine and let tomorrow take care of itself?

This is an admirable and relaxing state to be in – once in a while! However, if you have any ambitions, children, interest in the state of the planet, or even just a job, you need to shift gears and move your mood upwards from time to time. If you believe that you are worth more than a glass of wine and a pleasant meal, you need to find ways to motivate yourself and take action when you need to.

MoodMapping helps you to see where your energy is, so that you can fine-tune it. Ideally, you want 'action' to maintain peak performance. Then, as you finish work, head into calm to relax and recover in time for the following day.

Strategies to shift from Calm to Action

All five keys to mood can play a part here. Let's look at the best ways to get your relaxed self up and going.

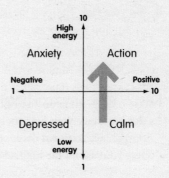

Key 1: Your surroundings

1. **Get stimulated!** It is easy to get too comfortable! The nineteenth-century poet Kahil Gibran, wrote, 'Verily the list for comfort murders the passion of the soul'. Wordy, perhaps, but he's spot on. Being too comfortable means that we lose the passion and motivation that drives us. Calm is fine and relaxing, but if you are always calm, nothing gets done!

2. **Find somewhere with plenty of energy.** You'll pick up the buzz and become stimulated. Choose a busy shop, a sales office, a railway station, or a bustling market. Just being around busy people can wake you up. Working in a busy office is more stimulating than working somewhere people have a more casual approach. We have a natural instinct to join in and if everyone around us is busy, we can feel left out if we have nothing to do. Whenever people get together, the energy level tends to rise. A buzzing environment helps you motivate yourself to get going.

3. **Go bright and light.** Look for rooms with plenty of light, high ceilings, bright colours, lively music, plenty of chat and movement, and lots of stimulation. All of these things will increase your energy levels – naturally! There is no doubt that our environments have a significant impact on the way we feel, and when there is a buzz or a hum about, our moods vibrate accordingly.

4. **Tap your feet.** To lively music, of course! Listening to rock music or hip hop may not be everyone's cup of tea, but it does wake you up and get you in the mood to work harder. If you drive to work, put on some lively music loud and get the beat going!

Key 2: Your physical health

1. **Get moving.** If you find yourself getting too comfortable, get up off the sofa, or swap your yoga posture for a bicycle. Exercise gets your blood moving, and fills you with energy.

2. **Eat a healthy breakfast.** Eating breakfast in the morning gives you energy to get you moving. Our bodies need fuel in order to operate at optimum level.

3. **A caffeine boost.** Although this isn't ideal for anyone who is sensitive to caffeine, a single cup of tea or coffee can give you the boost you need to start your day with a bang.

4. **Get some sleep.** Although it may sound odd to suggest sleep if you are experiencing low energy, it's a proven fact that you'll find it harder to raise any energy or motivation if you are tired.

5. **Walk in the morning.** Get up early one or two mornings a week and go for an early morning stroll – or even a run. There is something beautiful about the world before everyone gets up, when the streets are empty and it is just getting light. The energy you generate will last the rest of the day.

Key 3: Your relationships

1. **Surround yourself with do-ers.** It's impossible to sit calmly when you are surrounded by motivated, energetic people. You'll help each other to go that extra mile, and your collective energy will create a buzz that will keep you all firmly in 'Action'.

2. **Choose a good boss.** A good manager motivates his staff, and gets a positive energetic mood in the office. When you are looking for a job, you need to see whether your prospective boss could inspire you to produce your best performance or whether you would be able to get away with doing second-rate work. Although it might seem easier to work for an easy-going boss, you will do your best working for someone who has high expectations of you. What's more, you'll benefit from their positive energy.

3. **Find a buddy.** Friends who can help one another are ideal for creating the right motivated energy! Not only do people tend to operate better in teams, when there is a shared purpose, but a little healthy competition also helps to improve your mood. Push one another to greater successes, or spark ideas off each other. If you share a common goal, you'll find your energy levels soar.

Key 4: Your knowledge

1. **Self-talk, and talk** ... Positive, motivating self-talk can get you up at 6 a.m. on a cold winter morning, and it will also make sure you meet your deadlines. Use your self-talk to nudge yourself into action. Eventually, your brain will listen, and your body will follow suit.

2. **Find the right level of encouragement.** It is important to learn the skill of giving yourself encouragement, to keep going when you are tired or when you would rather be doing something else. For example, you may feel tired and believe that you are taking far too long to accomplish something. There are definitely times when it is right to listen to your body and rest, but, equally, there are also times when the only way forward involves pushing ahead, regardless of how you feel. Remind yourself of past successes, and how good you will feel when you've accomplished your goal. If you want to do well, you have to be prepared to work hard.

3. **Remove distractions.** If you know what diverts you, get rid of it so that you have no choice but to get down to work. For example, turn off your email and set the phone to answering machine when you have an important piece of work to do. Working efficiently and keeping yourself motivated involves full concentration.

4. **Listen to motivational tapes.** There are lots of tapes on the market, by gurus such as Anthony Robbins, Zig Ziglar and Steven Covey. Just hearing these guys talk can raise your energy levels. What's more, they have plenty of ideas that will get you going.

Key 5: Your nature

1. **Set your priorities.** When you live according to what you believe is important, and you are at one with what you are doing, you can enter a state of 'flow'. In this state, everything happens effortlessly and you achieve a very high level of performance. On those occasions when your values, your purpose, your being, your work and your talents align, it becomes possible to work at a new and higher level and these are the moments of flow.

2. **Set some goals.** Always have two or three compelling goals that inspire you. These don't need to be immediate goals; rather, a list of things you'd like to achieve. Why not create a 'dream board', and cover it with things you'd like to do, see, experience and achieve. Cut out pictures of places you'd like to visit, such as the Taj Mahal. Or choose experiences, such as scuba-diving or even lying on the white sands of a Caribbean beach. If you have aspirations to find your ideal partner, cut out some photos of the person you think would fit the bill (being realistic, of course!). Your dream board will remind you of the reasons why you should get up and go.

3. **Change the way you do things.** Find new ways to do something you do everyday. For example, take a new route to work, choose a different place to eat your lunch every day, explore the streets near where you work, or read your newspaper in a different part of the house. Every little change represents a 'new experience', which breaks your routine and gives you new ideas to get you going again.

Strategies to shift from Action to Calm

Being able to manage this transition is as important as being able to motivate yourself to action. No one, not even Roger Federer, is a machine that can continue relentlessly, month after month and year after year. Without the ability to rest and recover, exhaustion sets in. Learning when you've had enough, and when it's time to retreat into calm is an important skill to master. Keeping an eye on your MoodMap is one way to gauge what's going on. If you've been up in that upper-right-hand quadrant for the whole day (or longer), it's time to head downwards. Here's what you can do to get there.

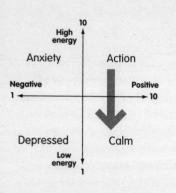

Key 1: Your surroundings

1. **Look for calm.** Peaceful and quiet surroundings can be the perfect antidote to a hectic day in sales, the Emergency Room, or in the office. For example, you might walk back through the park on your way home, to begin the process of relaxation. Find a way to separate work time from 'you' time, so that you are in a good frame of mind to relax.

2. **Soothing sounds.** Calming music, by a composer such as Debussy, Brahms, John Barry or even Celine Dion, can help you to bring down your energy levels. Just as you listened to rock on the way to work, you can listen to someone quieter on the way home. iPods are great for this. Have your 'going to work' play list, and another for unwinding after work.

3. **Invest your time in a good film.** Films can help you relax by taking you on a 'mood' or emotional journey. You'll switch off from the stresses of the day, and forget about work and anything else that's keeping your mind spinning.

4. **Find some water.** Being close to water – for example, sitting quietly by a river – has a wonderfully soothing effect on the mind. Water has proven therapeutic effects, and can be enormously calming. If you don't live anywhere near a water source, why not buy a little fountain for your garden, balcony or even sitting room?

Key 2: Your physical health

1. **Let off some steam.** Physical exercise helps the body to relax. How fit you are and how you respond to exercise determines whether you will respond better to a vigorous workout or a quiet walk.

2. **Sweat a little.** A sauna is a great way to relax, and it can help you literally to sweat out your problems. The heat will encourage your muscles to relax and release stored tension and discomfort.

3. **Some simple stretches.** A yoga class, or even just some stretching in the comfort of your own home will help to ease the tension out of your body, and encourage profound relaxation.

Key 3: Your relationships

1. **Keep your communication gentle.** If you are buzzing with energy or raring for an argument, you'll only feed 'action'. Aim for a quiet conversation with a calm friend, and avoid any topics that will raise your blood pressure or get your adrenaline flowing.

2. **Always say a nice goodbye.** No matter what has happened throughout the day, a polite and friendly goodbye helps to smooth over any tensions, and releases everyone for the remainder of the day or night. Hard feelings have a habit of building up if they aren't addressed, which can make you

anxious and distressed. Leaving things on a positive note goes some way towards alleviating potential problems.

3. **Never sleep on a quarrel.** Even if you have to bite the bullet and apologise, it's better to clear the air and remove the tension than to wake up the following morning with a battle on your hands. Furthermore, no one can sleep well with a row brewing, which will simply make things worse.

Key 4: Your knowledge

1. **Keep your head.** Perhaps more than any other strategy, self-talk can help you to be calm when you wish – regardless of what is going on around you. Rudyard Kipling sums it up in his poem 'If': 'If you can keep your head whilst all around you are losing theirs ...' Talk yourself into it – literally. 'I am *calm*!'

2. **Reassure yourself.** The habit of calm starts early, when parents comfort their children and calm them down. Once a child learns this pattern of behaviour, it can be used again and again. Being able to reassure yourself that the storm is not so frightening, that the worst-case scenario is not so terrible, and that you have done your best regardless of what happens is an important tool in managing mood.

3. **Pat yourself on the back.** Make sure you say 'well done' to yourself when you have worked hard all day, or, indeed, achieved anything at all. Even if no one else notices, you owe it to yourself to show a little appreciation for what you've managed to get done. Even if it's only you apparently noticing your efforts, your brain will respond positively to praise, and will be encouraged to repeat the performance the following day – and maybe even for longer!

Key 5: Your nature

1. **Accept.** Being calm is about accepting that you can do your best but not control every variable and every roll of the dice. It is about accepting that you have done what you can, and that there is nothing more you can do. The rest is out of your hands. By accepting what is going to happen, you can let go. Sometimes you have to stop plugging away and just see what happens. We can never control every aspect of our lives, and acknowledging this from time to time can be a massive relief.

2. **Be comfortable with yourself.** The ability to be calm depends on being comfortable with who you are, at peace with yourself and having a clear conscience. There is no point expecting yourself to be someone you are not. For example, if you are someone who prefers your own company, you may never be completely comfortable at the centre of a group. This is neither good nor bad, nor is it right or wrong. It's just a reflection of the person you are. Coming to terms with that is undoubtedly calming, as you let yourself off the hook.

3. **Learn to push the 'calm' button.** Being able to calm down is as important a skill as being able to rev yourself up for action. It is important to see rest as fulfilling your need for restoration and relaxation. It's not lazy to relax. Jack Black describes this well in his book *MindStore*. He believes that rest time is a time for idle creativity, to use your curiosity and pursue something just because you are interested in it. Hobbies are great ways to relax, whether it is fishing or tapestry, they can be creative ways to give yourself a different view of life. What's more, they can become instant 'calm' buttons when you need them most.

😟 😊 **Day 14** Exercise

Experiment with ways to move from Action to Calm, using your MoodMaps to judge the effectiveness of each.

• Find three different ways to get home from work. Which is the most calming? Perhaps catching the train might be better for you than driving in rush-hour traffic?

• When you walk in the front door, change what you normally do first. Instead of going to your answer machine to check the messages, go out into the garden to see if any new flowers have bloomed during the day, if any plants need water, and what changes have occurred since you were last there.

• Spend an hour in the evening trying something you wouldn't normally do: draw a still-life group of objects; bake bread; or reorganise your drawers, sorting your T-shirts and sweaters according to colour.

Come up with three strategies of your own for shifting Action to Calm. Think of strategies for a range of different situations. In the next chapters, you will learn how to use them to affect not only your own mood, but also those of the people around you.

Well done! You are now a fully qualified MoodMapper! Not only can you map your own moods, but you can teach other people how to map their moods, too. You can also use the tools at your disposal to gauge the moods of other people, and shift them as appropriate.

When you have all four moods at your disposal, you have a flexibility that will give you an unfair advantage in any situation. Remember that your mood is not *you* – it's just the way you feel in the moment. By understanding you are not your mood, but that your mood is there to serve and inform you, you can start to rise above your circumstances. You can do more than using the easiest and most convenient way to feel good. Instead, you have the tools you need both to monitor your progress, and to progress!

By now, you'll have a notebook brimming full of strategies and exercises that will improve your mood. You may also want to share them with others, to help them learn to control the way they feel as well. And you'll be amazed by the number of ways that you can use MoodMapping in everyday life – in your job, your relationships and your personal time. You can use it to shift your own mood, change the mood of a meeting, encourage healthy, happy behaviour in your children, or even manage the pupils that you teach. You can use MoodMapping to motivate yourself and others to achieve anything you want from life.

Next, we'll go on to look at the nitty-gritty details of mood, and examine how you can use MoodMapping in your interactions with others, and also use it to get the most from everyday life. We'll look at how personality affects mood, and perhaps go some way to explaining why you are the way you are. And if you suffer from more serious mood disorders, we'll be looking at those too, and working out the best ways to ensure that your disorder becomes order.

MoodMapping is new! Although it is exciting to learn something new, it is also hard work. Well done! Lift your arm straight up above your head, bend it at the elbow and pat yourself on the back for having done so well.

Moods and your personality

Now that you've worked through the 14-day programme, you'll be well on your way to mastering your moods. MoodMapping is a skill for life, and as long as you regularly take the time to map and gauge your moods, you'll find it much easier to control them, and experience optimum health and well-being.

There are, however, a few other factors that influence our moods and the way we feel, and over the next few chapters we'll look at them in detail. Here, we'll start with personality – and, in particular, the four 'matrix personalities' – which can make a difference to how you react, what you do, and, of course, your moods.

Unlike our moods, our personality is the part of us that stays the same from one day to the next, and over time. It is the part that defines us, and makes us who we are. Our personality is something that people come to recognise about us. For example, Martha might always be the 'life and soul of the party', Keith could 'always organise people' and George is the 'strong silent type'. Our personalities tend to remain the same, even if our moods shift.

Personality underpins mood, and it goes some way to explaining why some people are able to carry on regardless of how they feel, and others need to feel good before they can start. Mood shows how much energy and how good or bad you feel. It depends on your surroundings, physical health, relationships, knowledge and nature.

The four matrix personalities

Knowing your 'matrix personality' helps you to understand why you respond in the way you do, and also gives you some insight into how other people think and operate. With this knowledge, you can help to establish which type of people you can work with most comfortably, what type of work is likely to suit you best and, perhaps most importantly, which person will suit you best for a life-long partnership.

Why? Because some matrix-personality combinations always seem to get along, whereas others rub each other up the wrong way. Personality clashes are a major and avoidable stress. But when people get along, relationships are healthy, creative and exciting. Let's look now at the four personality types and decide which one you are.

- **Bold extroverts**. Extroverts are easily recognisable in public life. They talk the talk, can be charismatic or entertaining, and they are 'people people', who make excellent managers and politicians and can be relied upon to find the right words for the occasion. Examples of bold extroverts are Alan Sugar, who has made the job interview public entertainment; Tony Blair, who could always find the words for the moment, as could Margaret Thatcher and Bill Clinton, and as can Barack Obama; Stephen Fry and Derren Brown are both first-class, witty entertainers.

- **Shy extroverts**. These are natural talkers and naturally empathetic, but also wary, preferring to check a situation out before putting their toe in the water. They are, therefore, rarely seen in public life. Shy extroverts are gentle, people-focused and easy to talk to. Some good examples include Louis Walsh, Felicity Kendall, Rory Bremner and Cesar Millan (the Dog Whisperer). This group is the hardest to find in public life, because, in general, the shy extrovert personality is happier to stay behind the scenes.

- **Bold introverts**. Their boldness reflects their ability to get things done without a great deal of fuss, regardless of what people around them think or say. They tend to be people of few words, and are primarily interested in focusing on their work and doing it. They take their responsibilities seriously, have strong values and do not like to compromise or negotiate. They do what they say they will do, and expect the same of others.

Bold introverts with whom you might be familiar include Winston Churchill, whose determination and focus on the outcome of the war enabled Britain to emerge victorious. He had been suspicious of Germany for many years, and his opinion was not affected by what other people thought. Al Gore, John McCain, James Dyson (the successful entrepreneur who focuses on redesigning and producing the best products in the business), and Ranulph Fiennes (the Arctic explorer who is determined to do what he sets out to do, regardless of personal cost and focuses on the task rather than his audience) are all good examples.

- **Shy introverts.** Like shy extroverts, these are keen observers of people and situations. Shy introverts tend to observe before they act, they like to check out the situation before going ahead. Their shyness separates them from the everyday hurly-burly of life. They tend to be more focused, more creative and less open to negotiation than their shy extrovert cousins. Like shy extroverts they are not often seen in public life. Examples include Prince Charles, Simon Cowell (whose main strength is his ability to see talent), Michael Jackson (who lived in his own world), Gordon Brown, Elizabeth Taylor, Princess Diana and Michelle Obama.

Which matrix personality are you?

There are three approaches to discovering your matrix personality, and we'll look at those now. If you find that you come up with a different personality type for each approach, use your common sense to work out which type best fits your personality. There are no right or wrong answers here, and you will probably have a clear idea of your type as you move through the questions.

Approach 1

Below are four sets of words that can be used to describe people. Of the four boxes, which best describes you? Where do you fit most naturally? Individual words can potentially apply to everyone – for example, most of us can be diplomatic when we need to, or have the potential to be a team player. There is no doubt that most of us have a mischievous streak from time to time, and can be shy in some circumstances. But each box will give you an overall feeling for each personality type, so choose the box that contains words that best describe you overall. Are you A, B, C or D?

A

assertive	diplomatic
people-focused	friendly
self-confident	influential
good talker	popular
responsible	expressive
optimistic	able to recognise patterns

B

observant	curious
mischievous	wary
supportive	empathic
cooperative	warm
lateral thinker	intuitive
people-focused	shy

C

direct	decisive
independent	determined
responsible	confident
just and fair	logical
creative	goal-orientated
self-motivated	team player

D

romantic	intuitive
observant	cautious
problem-orientated	thoughtful
engaging	enigmatic
concerned	attentive
analytical	sensuous

You probably won't be surprised to see how the boxes match up:

A – bold extrovert
B – shy extrovert
C – bold introvert
D – shy introvert

This table is about 85 per cent accurate in identifying matrix personalities, so you should be beginning to have a clear idea of your type.

Approach 2

There are two main axes that determine your matrix personality. This approach looks more at how your mind works rather than focusing strictly on your personality. But it can be remarkably accurate.

- **Axis one:** This relates to thinking or talking, and it is designed to assess whether you prefer to think first and *then* express your ideas, or whether you like to work out what you think through talking and discussion. This doesn't mean that 'talkers' don't think, or that 'thinkers' cannot be good talkers. Instead, this axis looks at how your mind works. Do you prefer to talk to people about what you need to do? Or do you like to think about what needs doing and have your ideas straight before you talk to anyone else? Introverts think first, and then talk and express their ideas. Extroverts like to talk through a problem and reach their solution through discussion.

- **Axis two:** This axis relates to 'doing' or 'being', and 'observing'. People tend to fall into one of two categories. The 'do-ers' approach a problem by getting on and doing something about it. 'Be-ers' or 'observers' assess a situation, see what's happening, and then take action if necessary. This doesn't mean that 'do-ers' move into every situation regardless of the consequences, or that 'be-ers' never take action. This relates to your preferred first stance. So, do you like to make sure that things are done as soon as possible? Or do you prefer to wait until you've seen how the land lies, and have taken time to make a plan of action? Bold people tend to take action; shy people prefer to assess the potential consequences before doing something that might make things worse.

Next, you can plot on a line where *your* individual personality falls. Mark a cross on each of the two lines below. One relates to whether you prefer thinking to talking, and the other relates to being a 'do-er' or a 'be-er'. 'Inward' refers to the way you prioritise your thinking and feelings, whereas 'outward' refers to the way you prioritise your impact on the environment. Talking is an 'outward' communication, whereas 'thinking' is more of an 'inward' or 'internal' action. 'Doing' has a direct impact on your environment and everything in it, while 'being' is simply existing – or observing rather than getting on and acting.

Place a cross where you think you fall on the axis. There is no right or wrong answer, and most people tend to sit more on one side than another. If you tend to think before you speak, put your cross on the left-hand side. If you tend to think as you are speaking, and use conversation to work things out as you go along, you are on the right-hand side of the line. If you aren't entirely sure, you'll probably find that you sit somewhere near the midline. You may, for example, be a talker, but you may also think a lot!

The closer your cross is to the midline, the more balanced you are likely to be.

INWARD		OUTWARD
THINKING	<·····················|······················>	TALKING
BEING	<·····················|······················>	DOING

Let's say you are a deep thinker, but not much of a talker. You also prefer to watch what is happening, although you can get out there and do what you have to when necessary. Your matrix might look like this:

INWARD		OUTWARD
THINKING	<····X·················|······················>	TALKING
BEING	<·········X···········|······················>	DOING

Alternatively, you might be a great talker, but have always preferred to discuss what needs doing, and then get on with it. Your
matrix might look like this:

INWARD		OUTWARD
THINKING	<···**x**······>	TALKING
BEING	<·····························|···········**x**··········>	DOING

Finally, this is *my* matrix, with lots of talk and not much to show
for it!

INWARD		OUTWARD
THINKING	<·······················|·······**x**················>	TALKING
BEING	<·····**x**·················|·························>	DOING

From your matrix, you can work out which personality type you
are.

Talking + doing   = bold extrovert
Talking + being   = shy extrovert
Thinking + doing = bold introvert
Thinking + being = shy introvert

Personally, I find that this approach is more reliable than using
words, in that it seems to get to the core of who you are.

Approach 3

This approach looks at what drives you. Each matrix personality
has a different driving force and different needs.

- **Bold extrovert**. Your driving force is 'give me more!'. You tend
  to have few inhibitions and believe that 'if one is good, two
  are better, and three is great – so let's have them all!' This
  approach is bound to make you the life and soul of the party.
  You need variety, excitement and connection.

- **Shy extrovert.** Your driving force is 'make me safe'. This means that whatever you do, you tend to worry about what might happen, and gauge your actions accordingly. You look around a lot before you act. You can easily become anxious, particularly if the people around you are arguing or hurt. You are good at calming everyone down and making things better. You need security and connection with people.

- **Bold introvert.** Your driving force is 'never good enough'. Whatever you do, you'll always find ways to do it better – which is both your talent *and* your torment. Your standards are high, and your determination to improve constantly can come at great personal cost – in particular, stress. You prefer work that is important in its own right, rather than being part of a process and you prefer varied work.

- **Shy introvert.** Your driving force is 'do it my way'. You need to have everything lined up and in order (in your order!) before you can get started. Your ability to sense the finest distinction between excellent and outstanding means that you are often critical. Like the shy extrovert, security tends to be important for you.

Confused?

It may take some time to work out your matrix personality, not least because you may never have thought of yourself in this way before. Perhaps you have a wide range of different behaviours, and don't seem to fit neatly into any category. And some people are simply adaptable, fitting in wherever they go. It is also possible that you have never been pushed outside your comfort zone, and without being challenged, have never had to summon up various characteristics of your personality.

Your circumstances may play a role in how you think and operate. For example, if you are still living at home with your parents, it's likely that you are living and behaving according to their rules and expectations. This is something that carries on far past the 'living-at-home' years, too. You could also be working in a job that requires you to adopt certain personality and behavioural characteristics. If you have spent a lot of your life not being 'you', it can be hard to find the real you.

Your matrix personality does not change, but it can take some time for the 'real' you to emerge. If you are stuck, go back to approach 2 for a minute. Do you prefer thinking to talking or talking to thinking? Do you like to get on with the job or prefer to make sure everything is in place before getting started?

If you don't seem to fit into any category, it may be that you haven't thought about yourself in this way before. This isn't a personality 'test', and you won't necessarily come up with an instant answer. This is about who you are inside, and you may need to think about this for some time before you can draw any useful conclusions. If you don't come up with an answer that you feel reflects *you* as a person, then come back to this in a few days and try again. You won't be surprised to hear that your mood can affect the answers you choose.

Personality and work

Your matrix personality influences what you do best. Read on for a quick guide to the best careers, jobs and ways of working for each personality type.

- **Bold extrovert.** You are at ease in front of an audience, motivating and inspiring people. You can cope with rapidly changing environments, tight deadlines and a wide variety of tasks. You are good in the media, politics, marketing and sales.

- **Shy extrovert.** You are at your best helping people to sort out problems. You are naturally caring and might be a therapist or counsellor. You know what appeals to people in a marketing sense, and you are a good communicator. You enjoy solving complex problems involving people. For example, you are good in a support role – talking to people on the telephone and finding out what their problems are. You are also good at jobs where you deal directly with the public and with children.

- **Bold introvert.** You are at your best in careers where there is a combination of action and structure, such as the army, law, medicine and even piloting an airplane. Alternatively, you like to be able to organise your own work, and work at your own pace to find useful and creative solutions to difficult problems without being at the mercy of a rapidly changing environment.

- **Shy introvert.** You are at your best thinking through complex problems within a relatively structured and sheltered environment, where you can be creative and are protected from too many external demands. You are naturally empathic, and good with people, especially in a one-to-one situation. You are good at understanding the law, and also in jobs that require a firm grasp of detail.

These are not hard and fast rules, but there is plenty of evidence to suggest that each personality type has certain strengths and, therefore, certain roles that are better suited to them than others. A workplace needs to be balanced with all four types of personality represented so, ostensibly, there is no reason why you can't turn your talents – and your personality – to any job under the sun.

Other people

With practice, you'll be able to establish the matrix personalities of the people around you. This helps to protect you in all areas of your life – from the salespeople who will say anything to get your money, from being in the wrong relationship, and from exhausting yourself in the wrong job.

Ultimately, all of us are good at disguising our behaviour, and adapting to the norms of society and the places where we work. It is, however, possible to work out roughly the matrix personalities of the people around you.

In order to find someone else's matrix personality, you need to ask two questions:

1. Does he or she think before they talk, or do they work out their ideas during the conversation?

2. Does he or she prefer to take action, or do they prefer to know what is going on before they make a move?

So, in summary, if you are primarily a thinker, you are more likely to be an introvert rather than an extrovert. And, if you'd rather take action rather than hedge your bets, you are likely to be shy as opposed to bold. Put these together, and you can easily work out your matrix personality! With this knowledge, you can help to predict how you – or anyone around you – might behave in any set of circumstances.

Once you know whether a person is bold or shy, or introvert or extrovert, you'll have some clues as to where they are coming from. For example, you won't be fooled by a bold extrovert's fine words. They are likely to be an experienced salesperson rather than your newly discovered best friend. Equally, you'll be able to develop an understanding of people's working methods, and respect their needs. A shy introvert will probably need more time to think things through and get it right.

If you are looking for a receptionist, you need someone who is a good talker. They'll need to be focused on people and be able to communicate quickly and easily. You might also want someone who is observant and will notice the needs of your visitors before they express them. This would suggest that a 'shy extrovert' would be the ideal candidate for the job. Are you a shy extrovert? This may be the type of job for you.

Similarly, if you are looking for a salesperson, you need to find someone who can both do what you want, while being a smooth operator and talker. Who is best for the job? A 'bold extrovert'. Are you one? Perhaps sales is your field.

A 'bold introvert' might make the perfect mechanic, who will simply get on with the job. And so on. You can create an effective team using the matrix personality types as your guide, and you can also ensure that you end up in the right job for you.

Personality and mood

Each of the four matrix personalities responds to mood differently.

- **Bold extrovert.** You tend to stay in the 'active' quadrant of your MindMap. Your enthusiasm is infectious and your positive, outgoing mood can easily dominate. You tend to put your mood out into the group. You don't tend to be overly concerned about your mood, and are eager to get on with the job at hand. This can, however, make you vulnerable to exhaustion, because you don't stop and take note of your internal warning signs. You are often guilty of relentless action, continually adding to your schedule without being aware of the toll that it may be taking.

- **Shy extrovert.** You are usually lively and chatty, but very aware of mood – particularly that of other people. You rarely impose your own mood on the group, but will try to calm and comfort people who are upset, and cheer up people when they are down. You are not normally too troubled by your own moods, because you can usually find someone to talk to who can help sort out your problems. You can, however, experience difficulties if you become isolated or lose your support network. Although shy extroverts can be quite lively and chatty, you generally prefer calm.

- **Bold introvert.** You are usually calm, and *stay* calm in a crisis. You are aware of your mood, but can generally work through how you feel. When you get the job done, you feel better. Because of the high standards you set for yourself, you are at risk of stress – particularly so when you are not able to work to the standards you want. And because you can always see a way to improve whatever you have done, you can set yourself up for a difficult life because you tend to believe that the things you do are never quite good enough. Your tendency to think rather than talk can also make you look self-absorbed. Bold introverts tend to be calm, and work best in that quadrant, regardless of what is going on around you.

- **Shy introvert.** Of all the four matrix personalities, the shy introvert is most at the mercy of moods. You are aware of both your mood and the mood of people around you. You are naturally empathetic, but your inward-looking nature means that you can, under stressful conditions, retreat into yourself. Your mood can become overwhelming – whether it is anxiety or depression – and you can become paralysed in a state of inactivity. You need to be aware of, and actively manage, your moods. As a shy introvert, you are usually happy to go with the mood around you, and prefer the action quadrant, because it is more fun.

Personality and MoodMapping

MoodMapping helps you to become more aware of your moods, and helps you to learn when you need to employ strategies to shift over to the right-hand quadrants of your MoodMap. Matrix personalities help you become more aware of how the people around you behave and understand the reasons why they respond in different ways. Different matrix personalities work better with different moods. This is particularly important in the world of work. If your matrix personality does not fit with the type of work you are doing, or the mood of your workplace, you may become bored or stressed. You may find that you work better in a different department or, indeed, in a different company altogether.

Matrix personality types are useful summaries of people, but they are not set in stone. Most of us are flexible, and can do most types of work when we need to. However, if you want to be outstanding and to make the most of your natural strengths, your matrix personality can help you to make the right career choices.

Moods and other people

Our lives revolve around interactions with other people, and moods are central to the way we interact. Our moods and the moods of others can impact on everything we do, which is one reason why it's important to get them under control.

Mood is an instant form of non-verbal communication. Even before someone speaks you can often tell what mood they are in. Pets pick up on their owners' moods, and children can work out their parents' moods long before they open their mouths. So knowing what mood you are in, and shifting it before it negatively affects those around you, can be important to keep your relationships and interactions up and running. MoodMapping increases your awareness of your own mood, and helps you fine-tune how you feel – and operate. In this chapter we'll look at how moods affect the people around you, and how to use MoodMapping to ensure that you and they achieve healthy, balanced moods.

Mood-matching

A peculiar event takes place when we first meet people – whether it's someone we've never met before, or an old friend, family member or colleague. Initial greetings are almost always high energy and positive. And then the mood shifts and settles at a point where we both feel comfortable. We effectively *share* our moods. So if one person is feeling particularly energetic, they pass it on to the people around them. If someone is low, they can bring down the level of the collective mood to some degree; but, because they'll benefit from the mood-sharing experience, they'll also find that their mood lifts. So mood ends up somewhere in the middle of the joint mood spectrum.

Feeling that you are part of a group is about sharing the common mood. Almost everyone has had the experience of feeling alone in a crowd, and that feeling almost always stems from not sharing the common mood. Some people are naturally charismatic and have the ability to impose their mood on a group or crowd and make everyone around them feel special. Others can be negative. They draw conversations to a halt, and change the dynamic by imposing their less-than-positive mood on the group.

When managing your moods and those of others, you'll need different approaches, depending on the type of interaction you have.

One-to-one

When two people meet, they may put their moods together and find a mood that suits them both. If one of the people has a stronger mood, his or her mood may be imposed on the other party. 'Do-ers' or bold personalities tend to have stronger moods than the 'be-ers' or shy personalities. Bold extroverts, with a dominant action mood, can be good at putting shy people at their ease. Equally, a chatty but shy extrovert gets on well with the calm but bold introvert.

Being with someone is not just about sharing a conversation, but also about sharing the same mood. This kind of interaction is difficult on the telephone and almost impossible with email or texting. In fact, you can only bring together your moods when you physically spend time with someone. Matching moods is an important part of building relationships and developing communication. When you share a mood, you change the dynamic of the interaction. You work at a pace that is appropriate to you both, and this new shared mood encourages confidences and a relationship that develops on a deeper level. Sharing mood encourages you to share understanding.

This premise is one reason why business people travel halfway round the world for a meeting. They need to understand each other and share a 'mood experience' in order to develop trust and find common ground. And when people fail to match their moods, they misunderstand each other.

MoodMapping helps build an awareness of your own mood and with that comes an ability to see where other peoples' moods are placed.

ELLEN

Ellen had used MoodMapping for about three months, which made her much more aware of both her own mood and the moods of people around her. She noticed that two of her colleagues sometimes argued about the most trivial subjects. By observing her colleagues and plotting their moods on a MoodMap during their exchanges, she noticed that their mood seemed to change just prior to these arguments. As they became livelier and more negative, they both began to be a little more aggressive and rude.

Ellen realised that if she could catch them before the mood changed, the arguments would be averted. So as soon as they became lively, she intervened by offering them a cup of tea or a glass of water. This distracted them from each other, broke the 'mood-matching' process, and allowed the collective mood to calm down a little. By tackling the situation early, she was able to manage the moods of the people around her.

Strategies for managing moods one-to-one

- Tune into the other person's mood by following his or her pace and tone with the pace of your language and your body movements reflecting theirs. If their pace is slower than yours, make sure you leave plenty of gaps in the conversation to allow them to keep up with you. If he or she is working faster than you, increase your pace to match theirs. Once you have your moods synchronised, you will be able to communicate.

- Once communication is established, you have a choice. You can stay with their pace or move to your own. If you want to calm someone down, gradually start to slow the pace by introducing slight pauses into the conversation and slowing down your breathing. Make sure that you still have their attention by continuing to listen and keeping your communication positive.

- Your words must match your concern and your intentions. If you say you want to sort out a problem, you must intend to do so. Much interaction is based on the little cues that we pick up from other people. If you are being false, the other person will sense it, and will not trust you. When trust is lost, the collective mood changes and communication is no longer possible.

- There are times when the other person's energy is so high that you have to let them burn some off before you can start to slow the pace down.

- If the person to whom you are talking is depressed, he or she may not be able to increase their pace because energy levels are so low. You will need to slow your own pace, leaving plenty of gaps in the conversation. Go at their pace, not yours.

MoodMapping shows you other people's moods as well as your own. When you meet someone, the first step is to observe how energetic he or she seems. Do they come bounding through the door, or walk in quietly? This will give you an indication of whether they are in one of the upper quadrants – anxiety or action. Next, see whether or not they seem happy or sad. Are they holding up their head, or looking down or about anxiously with their shoulders hunched? Do they smile easily or is there a pause? This should tell you whether they are on the right-hand side of the line, or on the left. You can now determine whether they are in 'anxiety' (high energy and unhappy), 'active' (high energy and full of the joys of spring), 'calm' (low energy but peaceful), or 'depressed' (low energy and clearly not happy). Having a rough idea of their mood can dictate your communication. It may, for example, be the wrong time to ask for a favour, or to pass on good news. Equally, it may be a great time for sharing a joke or making plans together.

Parents and children

Managing the relationship between parent and child can be one of the greatest challenges anyone can face. One of the best ways to make this relationship successful is to use MoodMapping. If a parent can manage the mood of his or her child, behaviour will often follow suit. If parents focus only on the behaviour instead of the mood behind it, chances are that things will escalate out of control, as parent and child become increasingly stressed by their failure to communicate and, effectively, 'match moods'.

The sight of a mother screaming at her child, and a child screaming back or crying is a classic example of both sides having lost control. Unrestrained displays of negative moods and emotions do no good to either of them. Both mother and child end up exhausted; their nerves are frayed and they feel bad about themselves and each other. And if there is one thing I know from my many years of experience in dealing with moods, it is the fact that the more we lose emotional control, the more often it happens. Patterns of anxiety, stress, anger and fear are laid down early in life. The longer these patterns continue, the harder they are to change. This is important, because too many parent-child relationships descend into complete disharmony when clashes become a habit, and because there is no effort to find the root cause, which is often *mood*.

More than any other section of the population, children respond to and reflect your mood. If you are feeling stressed, angry or even tired, your children pick up the mood and magnify it. Therefore, in order to successfully manage both the moods and behaviour of your children, you have to be able to manage yourself.

Calm is the key. If you can break the cycle of escalating stress, children will always respond. Therefore, when you are feeling stressed, the best approach is to step back, take a couple of deep breaths, and then work on your own state of mind. Acknowledge how you feel, and then take steps to relax, as discussed. You'll find that this approach has a direct impact on your child's mood. When you are calm, calm ensues. One way to change the dynamic and the collective mood of any encounter is to whisper rather than shout. Like all loud noises, shouting can shift any mood into anxiety or even anger. Similarly, soft sounds can be soothing and draw you both back into the calm quadrant of your mood map. It is impossible to row in a whisper. What's more, if you suddenly start whispering, your child has to calm down in order to hear what you have to say!

Moody teens

As children become older, their moods become stronger and they develop more of their own moods and mood patterns. Children have moods of their own, particularly when they get overtired and cranky, but while they are still small, they tend to reflect the moods of the people around them. However, 'difficult' children are often those who have strong mood patterns of their own, even from an early age. This can be because they are lively and energetic, and consequently have higher energy levels than their parents.

Children suffer stress as much as the rest of us, especially if they become anxious about starting school or about their exams. This will show up in their moods. Instead of fitting in with the family mood pattern, children's moods becomes stronger and have higher energy.

Teenagers are, however, a different kettle of fish. In particular, hormone rushes and developing independence can cause teenagers to experience very unstable moods. This can place a great deal of pressure on a family, as it can seem impossible to negotiate their moods.

In fact, teenagers are often as distressed by their moods as their parents are – mainly because they are out of control. It is confusing to feel fine one moment, and then wildly angry, anxious or distressed the next. Low moods also characterise adolescence. For one thing, teenagers tend to have a different body clock to adults – a different circadian rhythm, which encourages them to go to bed later, and sleep for longer. Because they are lying in bed for longer, they may not want to do anything, even when they do get up. They may experience lethargy and even depression because of their low energy.

WHAT'S THE PROBLEM?

If your teenage daughter's mood is low and negative, you will *feel* it. You'll also sense her lethargy or her buzzy highs. It's a good idea to use this information to gauge her mood and help her stabilise it. In particular, if your teenager is depressed, it's important to work out the root cause. Is she stressed? Being bullied? Having relationship problems? Or perhaps indulging in drugs or alcohol? Is her diet OK? Is she getting any exercise?

Personality also plays a role. Although it is not as easy to work out a child's personality matrix – largely because children tend to be more shy than adults – you can usually work out a rough approximation. For example, if they like to do things with only one or two friends and tend to get absorbed in tasks, they are likely to be more introvert, whereas if they like to be with a group of friends, they may be an extrovert.

As parents, we have a responsibility to guide our children through to adulthood. They don't have the experience to understand or negotiate their own moods, nor do they have the strategies needed to change them. We need to help them recognise when moods become a problem, and provide them with solutions for making the changes necessary. A good place to begin is to work out if any of the five keys to mood apply. Apart from the obvious, what may be causing your child's mood problems?

Once you've ascertained the cause, you can then use some of the strategies suggested earlier in this book to keep things calm and to encourage healthy 'action'. In some cases, your relationship with your teen may be difficult. You may find that getting some advice and guidance from a professional will help her to engage with life, and inspire her to find happiness and contentment. Whatever the case, understand that mood swings and instability are a feature of the teenage years, and if you can adapt your own mood to fall in line with your child's, you'll be well on the way to keeping up essential communication.

Adolescence is stressful. Most kids are subject to a battery of examinations, and have to cope with changing roles and responsibilities, raging hormones, budding sexuality and independence, peer pressure and everything else. It's not surprising that many adolescents feel out of control, and even depressed.

The best way to keep the communication channels open is to lower your energy to fit your teenager's. If you are a high-energy person, this can prove to be quite a challenge. But your high energy will irritate your low-energy teen. In order to establish the correct dynamic for successful interaction, you have to mood match. In other words, you have to consciously meet your teen where he or she is if you want to communicate.

Stress in kids

Stress has also become a burden for schoolchildren. It is a long time since anyone said that schooldays are the happiest of our lives. Today, with continual assessments and examinations, over-scheduled lives, poor diets, inadequate exercise, overstimulation from phones, computers, iPods and the like, and even broken families, the pressure is on! Stress causes similar problems in children as it does in adults, leading to unstable moods, exhaustion, burnout and depression. This can disrupt the mood of the family as much as any other cause.

Strategies for managing your children's moods

Many of the same strategies that work for adults also work for children. They too need to learn about being calm. Children learn MoodMapping quickly, and even very young children can pick up the skills to do it themselves. In fact, such a visual way of describing how you feel seems to appeal to children, who cannot always find the words they need.

1. **Make a calm time.** Turn off mobile phones, computers, TVs, radios, iPods, games consoles and any other distractions. Start with 15 minutes, and keep the conversation quiet. No shouting allowed! Reading and simple, calm hobbies can be actively encouraged. Most of all, just spend quiet time together. Spending time together is often a rare commodity these days, when families tend to eat dinner separately or in front of the TV. Quiet is even rarer. You'll find that everyone responds positively to this imposed period of quiet, even if there is some resistance at the outset.

2. **Make exercise a regular event.** A recent study among Harvard graduates showed that mental well-being in the elderly related, among other things, to the amount of exercise they had as teenagers and in their early twenties. Physical activity reduces stress, steadies blood sugar (a major source of mood swings) and increases energy levels. What's more, it encourages physical fitness, which encourages overall good health and well-being. Kids need an outlet just as much as adults do, so make sure they get one, even if it's just a walk, a game of footie in the park, a playful swim, or walking the dog.

3. **Create some physical space.** As your family grows up, the organisation of your house may not work as well as it once did. Teenagers need physical space and will not hesitate to take over yours. This can leave everyone feeling crowded – and stressed. Little ones, too, need space to play without feeling that they are distracting everyone or making too much 'mess'. It's worth thinking creatively about ways to give your family more room. Maybe your dining room is pretty much defunct, and can be turned into a 'kid space'. An extension, a summer house or even a redesign of the space you have now may be pricey, but it is worth making the investment for the collective sanity and dynamic of your family unit. Ideally, kids shouldn't spend all of their time alone in their rooms, so community space that is geared to their needs will help to include them in the family goings-on.

4. **Create a healthy snack drawer.** Kids need plenty of regular
    fuel to keep their energy levels up, and to encourage healthy
    growth. Good, nutritious snacks will keep their blood sugar
    – and mood – stable, so make sure you have plenty to hand.
    A good idea is to create a drawer or a shelf in the fridge
    where they can help themselves to whatever is on offer.
    Choose healthy, whole foods. Hungry kids will, ultimately,
    eat anything on offer, and if they have a choice they'll think
    they are in control.

5. **Talk!** Although this sound obvious, it's amazing how little
    time we often have to sit down and actually talk to our kids.
    Sharing your own experiences can help them learn. Your
    child's mind is a blank little slate, and everything you tell him
    or her and share with him or her will help to create the person
    he or she will eventually become. What's more, kids have
    problems, too, and making regular time to encourage them
    to express themselves can go a long way towards stabilising
    mood and nipping any problems in the bud.

6. **Listen!** All too often our minds are elsewhere when our
    children are talking, and we miss the little signs that all is
    not well, or the little insights into their world. Furthermore,
    children are not as accomplished with language as adults are,
    and often find it difficult to say what they mean. It can take
    longer for them to explain themselves. Listen carefully, and
    give them time to say what they are feeling or thinking. If you
    are struggling to understand what they are saying, paraphrase
    and ask 'Is this what you mean?' Most of all, try not to
    interrupt or pass judgement. Kids sometimes just need
    a patient and loving listening ear.

7. **Assess your expectations.** If your parents had high
    expectations of you when you were growing up, no doubt you
    found this hard to manage. Make sure you aren't doing the
    same with your own kids. Many parents are guilty of living
    misspent dreams through their children. Remember that

children are individuals, and need to be respected for who they are, not what they achieve. Some expectations are good – they encourage kids to set goals for themselves, and behave appropriately. However, if they are too high, you'll suffocate your child's natural spirit, and leave him or her prone to mood problems both now and in the future.

Group moods and leadership

Natural leadership is about managing moods, and a leader's mood inspires people to follow. In fact, it is natural for people to want to be like the leader. A leader captures the mood of their group and directs it positively. Tony Blair's speech on the evening of Princess Diana's death was an example of this. On the day of her death, restless crowds milled around Kensington Gardens and Buckingham Palace, not knowing what to think or how to react. This mood echoed throughout the country. Tony Blair gave a speech that was right for the moment. He summarised the feelings of the nation, and described Diana as the 'People's Princess'. As a natural leader, he was able to gauge the mood of the people, respond appropriately, and then, when the collective mood had been established, guide it to something more positive.

Team conflicts start when an appointed leader no longer controls the group's mood. Where there is no collective mood, then the individual moods of the group members can threaten to dominate the proceedings and undermine the authority of the leader. It is confusing to be in a group where moods are poorly controlled, because non-verbal rivalries are set up, and people bounce against each other rather than towards a common goal. Energy is wasted, and can spiral out of calm and active and into anxious and even depressed. Good communication, good teamwork, all evolve from good mood management.

MoodMapping can be used to map the mood of a group or a team. It makes explicit what a good manager already knows, and provides an objective measure of how the team functions overall.

There are two main ways to map the mood of a group. The first is for people to map their moods individually but simultaneously – perhaps at fixed points in the day, such as 10 a.m. and 2 p.m. The 'mood leader' can collect the MoodMaps of his team, and see how well the individuals share the common mood. Where one or two people are out of sync, this may indicate a problem. It is important that people are encouraged to be honest. There should be no 'penalties'. MoodMapping can be used to solve individual and collective problems, and should never be used as grounds for bullying.

The second way is to map the mood of the group as a whole. You can do this by encouraging everyone to put a cross on a MoodMap that has been hung on the wall. Ask each team member to put a cross where they *think* the group mood is. This exercise can help to bring problems out into the open, where they can be solved.

Strategies for managing group moods

- **Be calm but assertive.** A natural leader is able to listen and communicate with people, express their concerns with sufficient empathy, and take action. He or she produces a climate within which all four matrix personalities thrive, encouraging diversity, cooperation and balance.

- **Respect the dynamic.** If a group has been together for a while it will have its own dynamic. If a new leader comes in and tries to disrupt it too soon, the group will be upset, and hostility will often be generated. Stop, get a feel for the existing dynamic, and then match it. Only then can you begin to guide it in the direction you want.

- **Get some first-hand information.** There is no substitute for first-hand information. If you can find out about people's moods by talking to them in person, and then uncovering the causes of any mood problems, you are well on your way to encouraging the change you want to see. If you are working with people who are moody or difficult, it is often possible to shift their moods – which will impact on the whole group

– by uncovering the root cause. You can also employ mood-matching here (see page 208), which allows you to reach the same mood level, and then guide it onwards and upwards – or, in fact, downwards when needed.

- **Listen.** In some ways, working with other people is the same as being in the family unit, and listening is absolutely crucial to keep open the channels of communication. Listening to people makes them more receptive to change – including an overall change in mood and direction. What's more, you can ascertain any causes of mood problems in individuals, or in the group as a whole.

- **Be aware of your own mood.** You may be influencing the entire dynamic, because a good team reflects the mood of its leader. The first step in leading or being part of a group is to make sure your mood is stable, and that it reflects what you want to achieve. If you are stuck way down in 'calm' and lacking motivation, you will never encourage your sales team to get out there and sell. Equally, if you are working in an office of accountants, being in buzzy 'action' may actually dissuade people from giving their work the attention to detail that it needs.

- **Change the mood!** If you need to create a buzz and shift everyone into active, then turn on the music and use some of the strategies suggested on page 144. If you need to get everyone into calm, then make the room more peaceful. Don't forget to shift your own mood first!

Mood management is a basic leadership skill. Although a person can say the right words, unless their mood is in tune with their followers, they will not feel understood, and people will not willingly follow them. When the gap between a leader and their followers grows too wide, change becomes inevitable. The skill of the leader lies in being able to reflect, express and shift the mood of their followers and being trusted to do what he or she says they will do.

Managing moods
in everyday life

Once you've got to grips with the art of MoodMapping, you can use it to assess your moods and then change them into something more positive when required. There are, however, times when negative events seem to overwhelm our moods, making it much more difficult to find a balance and get back on track. In this chapter, we'll look at some common situations where moods can be a problem, and some useful solutions to keep your moods stable and positive.

Procrastination

Perhaps the most common and widespread problem that many of us face is procrastination. We put off a multitude of things because we simply aren't 'in the mood'. So when you 'don't feel like it', 'aren't in the mood', or decide to 'come back to it later', it's time to adopt these strategies to shift your mood and get things done.

First and foremost, remember that mood is a choice. You can change your mood to one that cries 'action!' Another alternative is to ignore your mood, and simply force yourself to do what you have to do – regardless of how you feel – and hope your mood improves in the process. Finally, you can do something else and hope that you will feel like doing it later. But, if it's one of those jobs that's been sitting on your 'to do' list for a long time, chances are that it will never get done. MoodMapping is the obvious solution, and that's why the first option is always the best: change your mood so that you are in the right mood for what you need to do. Relying on a change of mood to just 'happen', or trusting your willpower, is never going to achieve the results you want.

If you look back at the circle you drew on page 78, you will see the areas that are not so strong. These represent the parts of your life where you procrastinate the most. There is always a 'reason' not to do your accounts, manage your home or visit your relatives. It's worth noting that anxiety and boredom are almost always at the root of procrastination. Take a step back and look at what's behind yours.

The more you dislike a task, the better your mood needs to be in order to tackle it. If the task stresses you, you need to be super calm; if the task tires and depresses you, you need a mass of high energy to get it finished.

It may help to use your imagination to make your tasks more appealing. For example, instead of planning a budget that makes you feel like a monk, look at it as a weekly battle with the wicked retailers and the robber salespeople of the modern world. Completing your tax returns becomes a game of chess between you and the Chancellor.

Strategies to beat procrastination

These strategies should help to shift you into action.

- **Use distractions.** If you have to do something you hate, find something to distract or even reward yourself with at the same time. Listen to the radio or watch some trashy TV while you do the housework. Play lively music and dance while you dust! Read while you exercise on a stationary bike. Nibble on a tray of exotic fruit or dark chocolate when you are doing your accounts.

- **Talk to yourself.** Self-talk is useful here. Keep reminding yourself while you are doing the task that you will feel great when you pass the finish line. Remind yourself how much you *want* the end result. You can even talk yourself into doing something, much as you would convince a friend to do something about which she was reluctant. Nudge, persuade, and promise rewards!

- **Delegate.** If you really don't like doing something, and you are likely to do it poorly, you may be better off not doing it. For example, if you hate ironing and your house is beginning to look like a Chinese laundry, why not pay someone else to do it for you – or offer to do something for them in return. These days trading skills is a great way to ensure that you never have to do the jobs you hate. Instead, you could do some babysitting, gardening or even grocery shopping in return.

- **Practise getting yourself into the right mood.** If, for example, accounts make you nervous, use a meditation and visualisation strategy, where you imagine yourself calmly doing the job. Come back to the meditation every time you feel yourself becoming anxious. To begin with, you may only be able to work on your books for perhaps ten or twenty minutes before you become too restless to continue, but it will get easier.

- **Be patient with yourself.** You may find that your mood is fine when you start, but that it starts to slip after a few moments. You may become anxious or distracted, and find it hard to concentrate on the job. Remember that it takes practice to concentrate for long periods of time – particularly if you don't enjoy what you are doing. So do things little and often, until you get the job done. Keep coming back to it, taking small steps in the direction you want. It is better to do a small amount, feel satisfied and come back to it, than it is to exhaust yourself to the point that you never want to go near it again.

- **Coach yourself.** This is where your 'inner coach' can help you most (see page 151). Give yourself the encouragement you need to keep trying and the confidence you need to know that you are going to succeed. If your mood starts to slip, repeat the concentration exercise again.

Stress

Stress seems to be the 'must have' accessory of the twenty-first century. If you are not stressed – verging on burn-out – you are not living. Stress simply means that you are under greater pressure than you can cope with. The demands placed upon you exceed your capacity to meet them. In simple terms, you have too much to do, and too much on your plate. Everyone has a 'stress threshold', beyond which negative symptoms are experienced. Your stress threshold is unique to you, and there is no point in comparing what you can cope with to the coping ability of others.

Over time, stress drains your reserves and you begin to lose your resilience to stress of any description. In other words, the smallest setbacks become mountains to climb, and the most minor difficulties become major challenges. Eventually you will become worn out, and experience the symptoms of stress, anxiety, exhaustion, burn-out and, finally, depression.

MoodMapping helps you to pick up the signs of stress early, as your mood creeps towards the midline and you start to spend more and more time in the 'top left' quadrant.

There are only two ways out of a particularly stressful work situation, and they are to:

- Work more efficiently

- Do less

In a world made up of targets, goals and labour-saving gadgets, most people will already be working as efficiently as they can. Therefore, doing less may be the only option. And doing less means saying 'no'.

If your job is demanding, you may depend on good concentration and a near-perfect memory. You may need to be creative and focused. You may also need to be calm or energetic, depending on what you are doing, and consistently so. In other words, you will probably be required to have a stable mood pattern. However, early on in the stress cycle, all of these things begin to fail and your ability to do your job will be compromised.

Your job may not be the only problem. Stress affects the five keys of mood (see page 143), and the reverse is also true. Stress can come from many sources, including your surroundings, your physical health, your relationships, the way you think, and your basic nature. For example, if you aren't being true to yourself or living by your values, you'll be stressed. Stress spills from one area into the others.

If you are under stress, it is easy to forget what you know. Your memory is less effective when you are anxious. Even when you know what to do, it is harder to remember it! The more familiar you are with strategies to manage your mood, the easier you will find it to use them when you are having difficulties and experiencing stress. Under pressure people tend to do what they are used to doing – what is second nature rather than what is necessarily best for them and the people around them. If you become accustomed to using strategies to manage your mood, you will naturally do the right thing under stress.

Unsafe, unpleasant surroundings put people under stress and, under stress, people find it difficult to look after their surroundings. An untidy desk belonging to someone who is normally tidy can be an early sign of stress. Poor physical health reduces a person's capacity for work, while prolonged stress leads to a huge range of debilitating physical symptoms. Difficult relationships with your boss cause stress and affect the amount of work you are able to do, while prolonged stress can damage even the most solid partnership.

Working in the wrong job causes stress, while too much work, regardless of how much you like the job, leads to stress. The same goes for your relationships at home. If you are stressed, your closest relationships will feel the strain. If you are experiencing problems in these relationships, you'll undoubtedly feel stressed. Problems in the five key areas of mood can cause stress, and they can also be affected by stress.

Strategies to manage stress

Managing your stress levels is one of the most important keys to managing your mood. Here are some ways to keep things balanced:

- **Find the root cause.** Managing stress means looking at all five keys to mood, to see where the problems lie, and to work out which areas are being most affected and disrupted by the stress. When you get a clear idea of the cause, you can take steps to cope with it and to prevent it from affecting other areas of your life.

- **Keep problems in perspective.** Some things are more important than others, and your priorities should reflect this. A tidy desk is important, but it's not crucial as the company tax deadline looms. Similarly, a tidy home is great, but if you have three healthy, happy kids who enjoy exploring their environment, you'll have to decide which matters most.

- **Find or be a good leader.** Good leadership offers the strongest bulwark against stress. A good leader can sort out difficulties, set priorities and goals, and help people feel in control again. A leader who lacks these skills can cause untold damage to a previously well-functioning team.

- **Calm is the antidote to stress.** You cannot be both calm and stressed. MoodMapping can help you to shift your mood from anxiety to calm. Calm comes from acceptance. If you can accept whatever is going on around you without a struggle, you will be able to conserve your energy for those times when you need to move into action. A lot of energy is expended when you anxiously react to every crisis. In fact, the more energy you use when under pressure, the more stressed you will become. It takes discipline to separate yourself from the buzz around you, and to maintain your own mood regardless of the chaos. Being calm conserves your resources. For ways to move from anxious to calm, see page 143.

- **Learn to say no.** This is harder than it may seem, particularly if you take pride in meeting every challenge that comes your way. But if you are already doing more than you reasonably can, and your mood is being affected, then it's time to cut back. Saying 'no' takes practice. You must learn the ability to step back and objectively decide what you can and cannot do. Suppress the urge to agree impulsively, and be practical. It can help to consider what your best friend might advise in a particular situation. Take their advice.

- **Create a STOP list.** This is most useful if you find yourself barely able to cope. A stop list is designed to create breathing space, and it's the opposite of a 'to do' list. Write a list of things that you can ditch, even if it's just for a short period of time. Can you forget about the ironing? Answering personal emails? Responding to phone messages? Put these on your stop list, and keep them there until the dust has settled. This will provide you with some breathing space while you work out a longer-term solution.

- **Go part-time.** Money is a problem for lots of us, but if you can't work efficiently, you may end up losing your job and having none at all. It makes sense to pull back a little and consider part-time work for a period of time. Reducing the hours you work, even if it's for a temporary period, is an option that most employers will consider, particularly if you can back up your request with a letter from your GP or an occupational health physician. While your income is undoubtedly important, it is essential to value your health above money. A period of part-time work should help you to rest and recover your resilience, and it has the added value of giving your employer some continuity. It provides a compromise for people for whom work is their life.

- **Talk to people.** Good communication or knowing you are not 'alone' can help more than any other approach. Feeling alone can be the most stressful experience imaginable for members of a naturally social species. We need people around us to help us gauge our mood and test out our ideas.

Mood swings and unstable moods

Moods swing are common, and most of us will have experienced them at different points in our lives – when we are stressed, premenstrual, suffering from problems in our five key areas, or even just experiencing periods when we are out of control. However, success in any area of life, as well as happiness and well-being, depends upon stable moods. Feeling in control of your moods can give you the confidence you need to face almost any challenge.

Alcoholics Anonymous use the word 'HALT' to represent one of the major causes of drinking. HALT stands for hungry, angry, lonely and tired. We can apply it to moods as well. If you are hungry, angry, lonely or tired, your mood is likely to become unstable. It's amazing how quickly your mood can be affected by exhaustion, depression, alcohol, a poor diet and a shortage of positive, nurturing relationships.

By comparison, you can create a positive shift in mood – and keep it stable – by eating healthily, having good friends around you, getting plenty of rest, and taking time to relax. Moods are more stable when we feel happy, content and secure with our lives.

Checking for mood stability

You can use MoodMapping to assess the stability of your moods. Over one day, map your mood every hour and see how much variation there is between them. If you find that there is a lot of movement, your moods are not as stable as they should be.

By becoming more aware of your mood, and taking the simple steps described below, not only can you improve your mood, but you can also make it more stable. Only if simple measures fail might you consider professional therapy or even medication to improve your mood so that you can deal with any more serious underlying issues. These issues might be difficulties from your childhood, which left you with a lot of tricky or distressing experiences to process, meaning that you did not learn basic mood management skills as a child. Your mood problems may be long-standing, and you may require time to learn new ways to handle them. You may also need a lot of support to help you make major changes in the way you approach problems.

Managing mood swings

Mood swings can be addressed by using the five key areas of mood.

- **Your surroundings.** Too much stimulation encourages us to become hyperactive. Staying in a safe, peaceful and stable environment encourages us to keep to a daily rhythm, and allows the body to calm down. Too little stimulation and you are at risk of becoming bored. Spend time planning an environment that allows you to feel safe. It should have sufficient objects and detail to give you things to think about, but not be so cluttered that you can't think straight.

- **Your physical health.** A regular routine, with a bedtime at roughly the same time every night, a healthy diet, reduced intake of caffeine, nicotine and alcohol, and some regular exercise will help your body to stabilise, and return the status quo. Look through the various strategies in each of the sections on mood keys. Every single one of these will help you to keep your moods stable.

- **Your relationships.** Some relationships are naturally more stormy and exciting than others. However, a turbulent relationship, going from passion to anger and back to passion encourages mood instability. If your moods are unstable and you are in a relationship with someone whose moods are also unstable, there are going to be fireworks. The classic example of this is Elizabeth Taylor and Richard Burton. Almost regardless of how much you love someone, if you are damaging each other, you have to get out of the relationship or agree that both of you will work on your moods. In this situation you cannot do it on your own. Counselling may be a key, but you can also benefit from regular MoodMapping. Try doing it together, to see how far apart your quadrants are!

- **Your knowledge.** Your past experiences, especially where there have been times of extreme stress and anxiety, can make you vulnerable to unstable moods. Good consistent experiences help you to build up your confidence. Therefore, every setback should be considered a learning opportunity. When you realise that you can handle whatever life throws at you, you will feel more confident. In turn, this will help to build resilience and dispel the anxiety that underlies much mood instability. Looking back at your wheel, which areas were difficult? What can you do to improve the way you manage your weaker areas? Do you need more confidence around the home? Do you need more confidence in relationships? Would an assertiveness course help? Would a communication course help? Do you need to learn more about how money works? Do you need academic qualifications? It's never too late to introduce changes to your life. Learning is a positive, lifelong experience, and everyone benefits from expanding their minds.

- **Your nature.** Some people, especially those who react quickly to external events, tend to be predisposed to unstable moods. If this is you, go easy on yourself. Realise that you are doing your best, given the resources you have available. If you are naturally moody, you need to do more than people who are not to help stabilise your moods. It will take you more effort and you have to spend more time on it. Life sometimes is not fair! Just as some people seem to put on weight more easily than others, some people seem to be more easily thrown by events than others. This is the way it is. Once you accept it you can get on and manage the problem.

Managing mood instability depends on living as stable a life as possible. It is not possible to screen out stress, but by rebuilding your reserves and spending as much time as you can in a calm mood, you will find it easier to manage your moods.

EXERCISE

This exercise will help you to stabilise your moods using a visualisation technique.

Begin by drawing a MoodMap. Mark a cross on it at a point in the calm area, where you feel comfortable. Choose a point with enough energy so you are awake and able to concentrate, and with enough positive well-being to be happy but not unrealistically so. Mark your cross here.

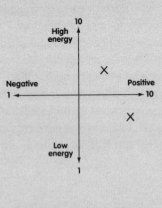

Two useful points for visualisation

Now, get yourself into a comfortable position, and select a piece of music that expresses the point on the MoodMap you have chosen. If you have chosen a calm spot, choose some soothing music. If you want something a little more energetic, choose something livelier. Gently close your eyes and start to play the music.

Now, visualise your MoodMap with its cross as you listen to the music. Picture it in your mind. Start to imagine a scene within you that expresses the point you have chosen. For example, you might choose a rocky outcrop in a calm sea with the sun shining down. You see yourself sitting on the rock looking out to the blue sea. Breathe from your belly to a rhythm of six, counting one as you breathe in, two, three, four and five as you breathe out, and six as you hold the 'out' breath.

Use this visualisation to steady your mood. Keep reminding yourself of this quiet steady place and bring your mood back to that point. You can bring yourself back to this point two or three times a day, by reminding yourself that this is where you want to be. You can use this point as an anchor, a place to which you can return when you are unsure about how you feel, or want to shift your mood to somewhere more pleasant. You can also use it as a benchmark against which you can gauge your mood.

MoodMapping is a tool that you can use both now and for the rest of your life. On its own, it gives you a visual interpretation of your mood at any given moment, and provides you with a record that will encourage you to keep track of your moods. Combined with strategies to change your moods – to make them more positive, or more appropriate for the situations in which you find yourself – it becomes a powerful technique that can literally change the way you feel in almost any circumstances. You can use it to help other people change their moods, too, which can be invaluable when the moods of those around you begin to impact on yours.

It takes practice to master MoodMapping, and to interpret the information you learn and then apply it in the best possible way. It also takes practice to understand the whole concept of moods, but once you start, you'll notice them everywhere, and see how they impact on your daily life and the lives of those around you. Soon, you'll be able to note instantly what mood a friend, your boss, your partner or your children is experiencing, and have a necessary tools to help them feel great.

There is great comfort in the knowledge that you have the tools at your disposal to ensure that the impact of moods is positive and constructive. Knowing that you can manage your own moods, and achieve stability and balance, will allow you to meet challenges you never thought you could. If you are a parent, a teacher, a doctor, a businessman or -woman or even just a partner or a friend, your success depends upon your ability to manage the moods of the people around you. And in this sense, mood management is a new kind of emotional intelligence. A person's mood affects how they think, how they communicate and how they behave. If you are master of your mood, you truly are the captain of your fate.

Mood disorders

This is where I came in. When I finally accepted the diagnosis of manic depression (or, bipolar disorder, as it is now called) in 1997, I had to come to terms with the fact that I was suffering from a lifelong condition. My psychiatrists told me that I would require medication for the rest of my life, so my first reaction was to search for a 'cure'.

After nearly a decade as a neurosurgeon, I had seen the brain recover from devastating injuries. I couldn't believe that I could not recover from a mood disorder. I researched every journal and article printed to find the cause of bipolar disorder, but found little of note. No one knew what caused it and no one offered a cure. My psychiatrists must be right. Medication was about the only thing on offer.

Little has changed since then from a psychiatric perspective, but on the psychological front there have been dramatic developments. Therapy is now considered an essential part of treatment, including group therapy and cognitive behavioural therapy. And, thanks to ground-breaking initiatives by the Manic Depression Fellowship (now called the Bipolar Organisation) self-management is firmly on the map. Self-management of moods, which includes many of the strategies described so far, is the greatest breakthrough in the management of mood disorders in the last 30 years.

Finding that very little was known about mood 'disorder', I looked at what was known about mood 'order'. It was from here that MoodMapping developed. I realised that mood 'disorders' are extreme variations of mood, rather than being separate from normal experience. And for that reason, many of the strategies that are involved in MoodMapping can be used for more serious mood disorders, albeit with some alterations. In this chapter we'll look at some of the things that you can do to keep a balanced mood, no matter what your mental health diagnosis.

Chemical imbalance

Mood disorders are often described as being 'chemical imbalances'. What this means is that moods relate to levels of dopamine (energy) and serotonin-endorphin (well-being) within the brain (see page 37). Mood affects almost every activity, so it is not surprising that many conditions have been linked to disturbances of the dopamine and serotonin systems, including dementia, autism, schizophrenia and bipolar disorder. It's also not surprising that medication is so heavily used in their treatment, because it directly addresses these symptoms.

But what my research and experience did prove is that mood and its associated chemicals respond more to the five keys to mood than they do to drugs. By physically managing your mood, it is often possible to dispense with drugs entirely.

Bipolar disorder

Bipolar disorder is a condition in which people intermittently experience extreme moods, including depression, anxiety, hypomania and mania (see below). It is labelled Bipolar Type I if it includes hypomania and depression, and Bipolar II if the sufferer experiences mainly depression. The self-management approach is similar for both types, and includes MoodMapping to help monitor your mood, living a healthy life, and intervening to manage your mood – sooner rather than later.

Hypomania and mania

Hypomania and mania can be frightening, both for the sufferer and those around them. Energy appears limitless while reason seems to have departed. Sufferers rush from place to place, talking too much and being overbearing, with a flight of ideas, flitting from topic to

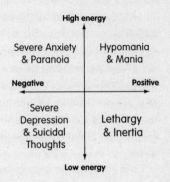

topic. In small doses it can be entertaining, but the person's mood can all too easily switch towards irritation and paranoia. Someone with hypomania can spend extravagantly and behave promiscuously. Behaviour is often impulsive, irresponsible and self-destructive. In a nutshell, it is dangerous.

As hypomania goes on to full-blown mania, sufferers may develop delusions, believing they are a famous and important person, have a special calling or special powers, or are even the Messiah. They can no longer be reasoned with, and they believe that you may be conspiring against them. Any criticism or attempt to control what they are doing can make them irritable and angry.

Psychiatrists tend to draw a line between a highly active mood and hypomania at the point at which someone can no longer control their behaviour and no longer understands the effect of their behaviour on other people. Before effective treatment, which almost always involves admission to a psychiatric ward, people in a hypomanic or manic mood sometimes die. Without effective sedative drugs, their continuous spiral of increasing activity can lead to exhaustion and even suicide.

Severe anxiety and paranoia

The everyday anxiety that we experience when faced with a potentially stressful event is not the same as the unremitting and intense angst that comprises severe anxiety. Severe anxiety affects every system in the body, including the ability to think rationally or to plan. It affects sleeping, thinking, walking, and the ability to do a job. Memory and concentration suffer. In the longer term, several studies show that this state of mind can damage the brain itself.

There are many physical symptoms associated with severe anxiety, including a racing pulse, constipation, diarrhoea, abdominal cramps and bloating, indigestion, chest pains, shortness of breath, dizziness and fainting. The constant stream of adrenaline from the fight-and-flight response overwhelms the 'housekeeping' part of the nervous system, and the physical body starts to descend into chaos.

Over time, severe anxiety leaves a person vulnerable to a spectrum of serious physical illnesses, and in this state of severe distress, people behave in ways that they might never consider under normal circumstances.

Relentless, severe anxiety can lead to paranoia, where the sufferer no longer trusts the people around him, and begins to believe that everyone is against him. In its most extreme form, everyone is seen as a potential enemy and the sufferer does not feel safe anywhere. On other occasions, paranoia may settle on one or two individuals, such as neighbours or relatives. Once severe paranoia has developed, it is almost impossible to communicate with a sufferer. Any approach, however friendly, is met with the irrefutable response: 'Well, you would say that, wouldn't you?'

Nonetheless, it can be too easy to dismiss someone as paranoid, without listening to what he or she has to say. A recent study of 'pathologically' jealous partners showed that a proportion had good reason for their jealousy; their partners were indeed unfaithful. Although a person's mood, thinking and behaviour can become extreme, there are usually underlying reasons – just as there are with *any* mood.

JERED

I was in clinic when a patient (I'll call him Jered) came in. Before he had even sat down, he announced, 'They write down everything I say'. This might have appeared bizarre, but the day before, his employers had sent me two large folders containing the transcripts of their telephone conversations with him. Sent, seemingly, to help me understand how mad he was ...

After a long consultation, it emerged that many of his problems related to the way his colleagues had reacted to him after he saw a counsellor in the 1980s. He was called names such as 'loony' and 'nutter', and had become increasingly isolated at work.

This degenerated into bullying and further name-calling, and his mental health deteriorated further. He had every reason to be paranoid! His employers were writing down everything he said!

I recommended that he be considered for redeployment in

company offices in a nearby region. I also suggested that a gradual return to work in an encouraging environment would help him. Some months later I received a report from his psychiatrist, commenting on his remarkable recent improvement. It seems he had been diagnosed with paranoia against a background of severe anxiety and no one had found out what had happened to set off these reactions. He had been depressed and anxious but this had escalated because of the way his colleagues reacted when he did seek help.

Although the consultation had not sorted out all his problems, by giving him the chance to get back to work and get back to a normal life, he had been able to start sorting out his problems himself. He had good reason to be paranoid! And although his reaction had been extreme, it did not mean that his mental health could not improve with the right support and encouragement. I don't know the end to this story, but I do know that once he started making progress, he kept on improving. It's difficult to know if bipolar disorder was at the root of his problems, or if he had developed genuine paranoia. And in a way that's irrelevant. He sought help, got help, and began to get better.

Severe depression and suicidal thoughts

Severe depression is difficult to describe to people who have no experience of it. Although it is part of the spectrum of milder depression, fatigue and tiredness, severe depression is an experience of different magnitude. It is a place where thoughts of suicide begin to look rational. For someone experiencing this type of severe depression, thinking becomes so distorted that even simple problems in everyday situations appear hopeless. Their energy is so low that getting out of bed can be a crippling effort. Life has lost all meaning; self-esteem is at rock bottom and feelings of worthlessness are overwhelming. It seems that no amount of reassurance has any effect.

Talking is hard for people with severe depression; it takes effort and does not seem to help. Yet, it does provide some comfort to know that the people around you care. This is the time when people need to know that they are not alone in the world.

Paradoxically, however, it is also the time when it is the hardest to make contact.

People often wonder what they should say to someone who is severely depressed, whether from bereavement or other reasons. The simple answer is that anything will do, but ordinary, everyday conversation is best. As long as communication is well intentioned, it is almost impossible to make a mistake. Even if your approach is rejected, it helps sufferers to know that another person cares enough to make the effort. We are a social species, and isolation is perhaps the worst fate that can happen to anyone.

Suicidal thoughts are almost normal in this situation, and if you are concerned about someone, it is always a good idea to ask if he or she has considered suicide. This may sound impossibly invasive, but anyone who has experienced these thoughts should be seen by a mental health specialist as soon as possible. Rest assured that you will not make someone think of suicide by asking the question, and you may well save a life by doing so. Anyone considering suicide or even entertaining suicidal thoughts needs urgent psychiatric help, and it's important that you help get him or her to a hospital, where professional care can be immediate.

Causes of bipolar disorder

As yet, no one knows the causes of bipolar disorder, even though there are numerous claims that a 'bipolar gene' has been found. As yet, no genetic marker has stood up to independent scientific study. Nonetheless, bipolar disorder does seem to run in families. Why and how are still unclear. We do know that the majority of people with bipolar disorder do not have close relatives with the condition.

Other causes include stress. Almost everyone I have spoken to with bipolar disorder had their first episode of bipolar disorder in extremely stressful circumstances. Later episodes seem to be triggered by less severe stresses.

Bipolar disorder can also start after head injury, treatment with anti-malarial drugs, particularly mefloquinine, head injury, childhood abuse, drug abuse, severe sepsis, ruptured appendicitis, toxic shock, exposure to organophosphates (pesticides), post-traumatic stress disorder, alcoholism and abusive relationships. It seems that any situation in which a person is highly stressed, either physically, mentally or biochemically, can in certain circumstances and in some individuals bring on bipolar disorder.

Warning signs

Warnings are the signs of impending illness and mean that you need to take action. These may be different for depression and for hypomania.

Typical warning signs for depression include tiredness, not wanting to go out, eating too much, not eating, losing interest in hobbies, and finding it difficult to get up in the morning. These may follow a period of doing too much, and it is important to understand the difference between tiredness, depression and lethargy. Tiredness needs rest, whereas depression also needs some strategies to improve well-being, such as meditation, massage, aromatherapy, music and going to bed on time.

All too often people increase their flagging energy levels by using artificial stimulants to get a buzz or a burst of liveliness. These include caffeine, sugar and processed foods. Sure, they work in the short term; however, they will leaving you feeling much worse when their effect wears off and, over time, they can play havoc with your health. The stimulation provided by these substances also keeps you going when your brain and body are crying out for a rest. If you are tired, there is a reason why. If you artificially stimulate yourself, you'll become increasingly tired and then exhausted. I have yet to meet someone suffering from depression who was not also exhausted. So that innocent latte may, in fact, be sending you the wrong way! The healthier and more natural your diet, the more you protect yourself from depression.

Typical warning signs for hypomania include being irritable, reduced sleeping, increased energy, thinking about lots of things at once, becoming slightly paranoid, not eating, eating too much, spending money, becoming promiscuous, speaking loudly, annoying people, and seeing 'special meanings' in events.

By knowing your own triggers and warning signs, you can re-mind yourself of what you need to look out for.

Strategies for managing bipolar disorder

The following should help to keep the demons at bay, and can be used when you experience warning signs. Better still, adopt them as a regular part of daily life to help ensure balanced moods and respite from episodes.

- **MoodMapping and mood-monitoring.** Understanding how you feel and what is contributing to your mood is essential. Unless you regularly check in with yourself to see how you feel, you cannot expect to stay on an even keel. Often just knowing where you are is enough to help you draw back and relax.

- **Calm is always safe.** One of the scourges of bipolar disorder is the idea that you can never be calm again. All too often, as your energy starts to increase, you start to worry that you are becoming 'high', and need to calm down. Calm is happy, albeit a low-energy form of happiness that is not widely advertised in our high-energy, stress-based society. Being calm and at peace helps the mind to heal. While you are calm, you are neither depressed nor hypomanic.

- **Choose the strategies that work for you.** Use the strategies that you have found in this book that seem helpful and keep your mood on as even a keel as possible. It helps to accept that different moods throw up different experiences, and this is simply the way it is. You can manage your mood to the best of your ability, but there may be times when you do not feel as good as you would like. As long as your mood remains within reasonable boundaries and you are living an emotionally and physically healthy life, your mood will improve.

- **Fish oils are essential.** Your doctor may even prescribe them for you. At present, because of the cost of getting a drug licensed, none of the companies producing fish oils have a government licence approving their prescription in bipolar disorder. There are, however, many, many studies showing their benefits. What's more, they are free from side-effects. If your doctor does not want to prescribe them, you can buy them from chemists or online. Two grams a day is the ideal dose.

- **Keep a regular mood diary.** Just as diabetics monitor their blood sugar, a person with bipolar disorder needs to monitor their moods, in order to take action before a mood becomes too extreme. It is easier to calm down from a little bit of excitement than it is from hypomania. This means not just checking in with yourself with regular MoodMapping, but also keeping a record of what is happening in your life. You can use your notebook for this, or a diary. When you find you are doing too much, slow down before your mood descends into depression – or becomes hypomanic when you continue to push yourself harder and harder in order to keep up.

- **Talk to other people with bipolar disorder.** Regular support meetings help you feel 'normal' and prevent feelings of isolation from setting in. You can discuss what you are feeling with other people who have similar problems, and swap strategies and experiences.

😞😊 Exercise

The key to self-management is knowing what can trigger an episode of hypomania or depression, and becoming familiar with the warning signs of an impending episode. Only undertake this exercise if you are feeling well and reasonably balanced. If you are feeling unstable, come back to it later on.

There are three parts to this exercise, and it can be done in your notebook. It may take a little while, but it's worth the effort. You may want to consider doing it with your partner, carer or a close friend or family member.

You'll need a notebook page or a sheet of paper that will provide enough space for lots of information. You'll be breaking your life down into five-year increments: 0–5 years, 6–10 years, 11–15 years, 16–20 years, and so on.

In each of these five-year blocks, write down the major events that you can remember, as well as anything that you can think of about your mood at the time. Were you depressed? High?

See if you can spot any pattern emerging. Is there anything that repeatedly made you feel vulnerable? Or that may have triggered your episodes? See if there is any link between what was happening to you, and how you felt.

A close friend or a professional therapist can help you make sense of your timeline if you find it difficult yourself.

The next step is to identify your triggers and warning signs. Triggers are those things that set off a serious episode of illness. They aren't causes, as such, but nudges that send the whole episode into action. For each event or episode, see if you can work out what may have triggered the illness, and what warning signs you may have experienced.

For me, the important triggers seem to have been immediately related to the loss of support from close friends that came with career moves, and also to stressful times in my career, such as changing jobs. Can you see what yours are?

The following is a rough outline of what I wrote about my own life.

AGE	MAJOR EVENTS	MOOD
0–5	Moved house at two years old, started school	Can't remember much, but I didn't like school
5–10	New school at age seven, put in a different class from the rest of my friends	Still didn't like school
11–15	Went away to boarding school	Still not enjoying school

continued...

16–20	Started university	Enjoyed university but didn't like the course
21–25	Started working as a doctor	Enjoyed neurosurgery
26–30	Worked as a neurosurgeon	Enjoyed neurosurgery although hard work and competitive
31–35	Moved to Edinburgh Bipolar disorder diagnosed	Didn't like the move to Edinburgh, worried about my career
36–40	Further changes in career and final episode of illness	Career changes may have been associated with illness

This is a brief summary of my own life. Looking back, I can see that one of my abiding memories of childhood was disliking school. I used to wonder if this laid the seeds for the bipolar disorder that came later on in my life; however, when I look back at my life I can see that my episodes were associated with my career. They came on when I was moving on to the next stage of my career, or when I was moving around the country, taking different jobs in order to progress. I'm certain that one of the reasons why I am no longer ill is because I am no longer chasing a career.

By looking at your own life in this way, you may see very clearly what triggered episodes of illness, and use this knowledge to avoid triggers – or learn how to handle them.

Conclusion

One evening, an old Cherokee told his grandson about a battle that goes on inside people.

He said, 'My son, the battle is between two wolves inside us all. One is evil. It is anger, envy, jealousy, sorrow, regret, greed, arrogance, self-pity, guilt, resentment, inferiority, lies, false pride, superiority and ego.

'The other is good. It is joy, peace, love, hope, serenity, humility, kindness, benevolence, empathy, generosity, truth, compassion and faith.'

The grandson thought about it for a minute, and then he asked his grandfather, 'Which wolf wins?'

The old Cherokee simply replied, 'The one you feed.'

Living a healthy life does not mean that you will never have another bad mood or a bad day. Instead, it means that when life goes wrong and your mood starts to fail, you know what to do. Mood management involves finding ways to cope, so that you will not be dragged down by the way you and the people around you feel.

MoodMapping is a tool to help you choose how you feel, every moment of every day and every year from hereon in. It helps you to choose the healthy alternatives rather than doing something that is easy and convenient. For example, once you know the impact of healthy food on your mood, you'll probably choose to make your own meals instead of buying something ready-made for the microwave. You will learn that walking up the stairs will help to lift a low mood, and that regular exercise makes you sleep better. Every time you map your mood, you'll find out something new about yourself, and learn what makes you go up and what brings you down. This helps to create a template for living, leading to stable moods. What's more, it gives you the resilience you need to come through whatever life throws at you.

It's important to remember that anxiety and depression are choices. There are times when it is appropriate to experience these moods, but when they stay around for a long time, and when they prevent us from living our lives to the full, it's time to take action. Moods need to be balanced and managed. If you are not managing your own mood, chances are that someone else is, whether that someone is your boss, your partner, the government or even the advertisers who catch your attention at every turn. If you aren't in control of your mood, someone else is making you feel the way you do – and, frankly, you are letting them! Getting control of your moods is uplifting and empowering; keeping control of them is life-enhancing.

Moods are infectious and we have a duty to the people around us not to poison them with our bad temper or annoy them with a mindlessly positive attitude. A strong collective mood helps pull people through bad times, while isolation from the group is one of the most destructive punishments there is. We are on this planet together and part of a greater tribe. If we all confidently managed our moods, the energy and happiness we could produce is fathomless. Moods spread, and as we interact, we share them. Your healthy, balanced mood can have an incredible impact on the people around you, and you can achieve so much more from your life on a personal level when you have your moods under control.

All of us want to be happy and fulfilled, and we want the people around us to experience the same thing. Mood is probably the most important element of being happy, and so it makes perfect sense to come to terms with the power it has over our lives, and the role it can play in ensuring that we live our lives to the full. MoodMapping is an essential part of the process of mood management. It provides us with the tools we need to understand our moods, guide them in positive directions, and nurture them so that they remain stable. And when that occurs, you'll find that your world is transformed. You will have the power to be you – not governed by the ups and downs of your moods, or those of others, but able to make choices that are right for you, *when* they are right for you.

Further information

Internet resources

Health & Diet

www.rawfamily.com
How one family switched to a raw diet and greatly improved their health as a result.

www.mentalhealth.org.uk/campaigns/food-and-mental-health
The Mental Health Foundation has a lot of information about mental health; this section is about the links between food and mental well-being.

www.sustainweb.org
A broad approach to food, health and lifestyle.

www.foodrevolution.org/index.htm
John Robbins writes about the relationship between diet and Western disease.

www.mind1st.co.uk and *http://www.vegepa.com*
More information about the benefits of omega 3 fish oils.

www.eatmoveandbehealthy.com
Paul Chek writes about the relationship between health, diet and physical exercise.

Personal development

www.anthonyrobbins.com
Anthony Robbins is perhaps the best known of the personal development gurus. His website gives an introduction to goal setting and some information about his programmes.

www.influenceatwork.com
Robert Cialdini describes the means by which one person influences another. If you want to learn marketing or just avoid being pressurised by salespeople, this is a good place to start.

Finance
Money education

www.richdad.com
www.conspiracyoftherich.com
Robert Kiyosaki explains the way rich people think about money, and how we can all benefit from their ideas. This is a good place to start your financial education.

www.moneysavingexpert.com
A fun website that brings you some good money-saving deals.

Psychology
http://psychcentral.com
http://psychcentral.com
A broad-based website that offers a wide range of information about different aspects of psychology.

Mental health
www.bluepages.anu.edu.au
Sensible information about depression; just knowing where you stand can help you deal with it.

www.mentalhealthrecovery.com
Mary Ellen Copeland has been teaching self management for more than 20 years. Her *Depression Workbook* leads the market, and she runs WRAP self-management programmes. Highly recommended.

Cognitive Behaviour Therapy
The Mood Gym

www.moodgym.anu.edu.au
Computer-generated questions that can help you deal with depressive thinking. This is a free programme that you can do for yourself and gives you an introduction to cognitive behaviour therapy.

www.mindapples.org
A fun blog, to which people contribute '5-a-day mind apples' (strategies to keep you mentally healthy).

Relationships

http://en.wikipedia.org/wiki/Emotional_intelligence
A quick summary of the concept of emotional intelligence, which shows that social skills and emotional skills are as important for success as your academic and intellectual skills.

www.workingfamilies.org.uk
Advice on keeping a good work-life balance.

Support groups

Bipolar

www.mdf.org.uk
The Bipolar Organisation runs groups for people with bipolar disorder, providing support and information. They also run mental health self-management courses.

www.standtoreason.org.uk
Stand to reason is an organisation that campaigns to reduce the stigma and discrimination that surrounds mental health.

Bereavement

www.crusebereavementcare.org.uk
Losing someone you love is traumatic and can affect your life for many years. This organisation offers counselling and support for those who are grieving and need some extra support.

www.moodmapping.com
www.matrixpsychology.com
Websites with more information about the psychological principles underlying this book.

Reading list

Self help

Diet For A New America by John Robbins, H. J. Kramer, 1998
A clear explanation of what has happened to our food supply and what we can do about it

The Natural Way to Beat Depression by Basant K. Puri and Hilary Boyd, Hodder Mobius, 2004
More about omega 3 fish oils and their benefits in depression and with other mental health problems.

Potatoes not Prozac by Kathleen DesMaisons, Pocket Books, 2001
An alternative diet-based approach to depression – let food be your medicine.

Healing Without Freud or Prozac by Dr David Servan-Schreiber, Rodale International Ltd, 2005
This book covers a wide range of therapies, backed up by academic studies which provide alternative ways, apart from medication, to manage your mental health.

Beyond Prozac: Healing Mental Suffering Without Drugs by Terry Lynch, Mercier Press, 2005
This looks at the social problems that inevitably accompany depression.

Manage your Mind by Gillian Butler and Tony Hope, OUP, 2007
Useful strategies and a practical no-nonsense approach.

The New Leaders: Transforming the Art of Leadership by Daniel Goleman, Richard E. Boyatzis and Annie McKee, Time Warner, 2002
How leaders use feelings and emotions to improve their leadership.

Awaken the Giant Within: How to Take Immediate Control of Your Mental, Emotional, Physical and Financial Life by Anthony Robbins, Pocket Books, 2001
A densely packed and informative approach to being the best you can be.

The Good Mood Diet: Boost Your Serotonin Levels to Lose Weight, Curb Cravings – and Feel Great by Judith J. Wurtman and Dr Nina Frusztajer Marquis, Rodale, 2007
Practical and helpful recipes with know-how behind them.

Gut Instinct: What Your Stomach Is Trying To Tell You – 7 Easy Steps to Health and Healing by Pierre Pallardy, Rodale, 2006
Practical and useful explanation of the link between the gut and wellbeing. Well ahead of its time.

Psychology and neuroscience

Neuroscience: Exploring the Brain 3rd edition by Mark F. Bear, Barry W. Connors and Michael Paradiso, Lippincott Williams and Wilkins. 3rd edition 2006

The Brain: Neuroscience Primer by Richard H. Thomson, W.H. Freeman & Company, 2000

Both books are relatively simple clear approaches to the brain, for the academically minded.

Psychology: The Science of Mind and Behaviour by Richard D. Gross
2nd edition
I prefer the second edition to the fourth, as it has more basic
psychology.

The Feeling of What Happens by Antonio Damasio, Vintage Press,
2000
This is a neurological explanation of what makes us conscious, again
for the more academically minded.

Index